Discovery-Driven Growth

A Breakthrough Process
to Reduce Risk and
Seize Opportunity

Rita Gunther McGrath
Ian C. MacMillan

Harvard Business Press
Boston, Massachusetts

Library of Congress Cataloging-in-Publication Data
McGrath, Rita Gunther.
    Discovery-driven growth : a breakthrough process to reduce risk and seize
opportunity / Rita Gunther McGrath, Ian C. MacMillan.
        p.   cm.
    ISBN 978-1-59139-685-7 (hardcover: alk. paper)
    1. Corporations—Growth—Management. 2. Organizational effectiveness.
3. Strategic planning. I. MacMillan, Ian C., 1940– II. Title.
HD2746.M34 2009
658.4'063—dc22

                                                                        2008041024

From Rita

MacMillan helped, too.

From Ian

To Jean, Sandy, Adam, Eric, KC, Milo, Faren,

in fact the whole gang

.

Contents

Part III
Making Discovery-Driven Growth Work for You

CHAPTER ONE

Driving Corporate Growth with the Right Disciplines

Despite its centrality, driving corporate growth is paradoxical—everyone recognizes its importance, yet it is easy to get it wrong. The result is that every day, in offices and conference centers, in meeting rooms and airports, anxious executives in well-established companies worry deeply about how they are going to lead strategic growth in their organizations. CEOs worry about how to deliver the growth they pledged to their boards, CFOs worry about how they will appease a growth-hungry stock market, and COOs and their direct reports worry about how they are going to deliver the growth targets that were promised at the last stockholders' meeting, while still retaining corporate efficiency. Our argument is that their worries are well grounded. The time-tested, comfortable approaches to everyday management don't work well in dynamic, rapidly changing, and therefore cruelly uncertain environments. Consequently, while many companies invest in growth initiatives, the results are uneven.

Why So Many Good Companies Fail at Growth

We've all heard many cautionary tales about well-managed and successful companies that stumbled disastrously when they tried to pursue opportunities for growth. Revlon's 2006 introduction and almost immediate abandonment of Vital Radiance cosmetics (a $100-million-plus flop), Michelin's 2008 withdrawal of the PAX run-flat tire system, and even fabled General Electric's exploration of new financial products are just a few examples of smart companies whose processes for managing growth seem to have let them down badly. But failing to grow is not an option. Today's core business is highly unlikely to be an engine of growth for tomorrow. Accordingly, investors will see companies without a compelling approach to growth as nothing more exciting than a ten-year bond.

For over two decades, the two of us have been studying why so many well-conceived, carefully planned growth programs go wrong and why so many good companies just can't seem to get traction from their growth initiatives. We've also gained experience with companies that are getting it right and enjoying the growth and prosperity that ensue. In our many years of working with companies such as Nokia, Air Products and Chemicals, 3M, DuPont, IBM, and many others, we've distilled practices that allow managers to choose better strategic growth projects, reduce the risk of these projects, and either execute them with relentless success or discontinue them at very low cost. This book is the result.

Our core thesis is that companies that use conventional methodologies to pursue exceptional growth are doomed to be disappointed. They will simply not be able to accomplish growth that allows them to break out of the pack and deliver exceptional results. Consider how IBM learned, painfully, that its one-size-fits-all management style was crippling its growth efforts and how the company needed to operate differently.

How IBM Learned to Use the Right Initiatives to Drive Growth

In April 2001 we were sitting with a few folks from the strategic planning office at IBM. As you'll remember, IBM was virtually given up for dead when Lou Gerstner was appointed CEO in 1993 and began what he later would describe as a transformation effort. Throughout much of the 1990s, the company focused on ripping out costs, fixing individual businesses, and generally getting its house in order. But that clearly wasn't going to be enough to restore Big Blue to its former glory as the most desirable of the blue chips. Despite sincere efforts, growth projects stalled, and Gerstner wanted to get to the bottom of it.

Strategy chief J. Bruce Harreld later recounted in a keynote address how the change came about:

> In the early summer of 1999, we had decided to go after a new business area. So in September, there is Lou Gerstner sitting in his office on a sunny afternoon and he sees a line drawn through the project on the budget. It turns out that the executive in charge had said, "due to our current cost pressures, we decided to cut back on those activities we decided to invest in in June."
>
> Lou wrote this note, in frustration. "I have had it," he said. "This is a bunch of crap for this big business unit to believe that this little thing is going to have any material impact on their results for June. I want you, you and you [the colleagues who were at our meeting in 2001], to understand what's going on here. There is something systemically wrong with IBM and how we manage that we can't embrace and stay with new investments for growth.[1]

What they found echoes the conclusions from our own research. Essentially, the techniques that IBM was using to manage its bottom line and drive efficiency—techniques that were working well for the core business—were smothering the new growth ventures. IBM executives started to explore new disciplines, new techniques, that could help the company nurture small growth initiatives without losing sight of its core business operations.

As Harreld later put it: "We needed different management systems with businesses at different stages of maturity. The new businesses, the growth businesses, needed to be protected and needed a different kind of management style. They weren't like our mainframe business."

The insight learned at IBM through many painful experiences is that you can't manage growth programs using conventional approaches. This single insight profoundly changed the way the company funds, structures, and plans growth projects, to the point at which IBM's emerging business opportunity (EBO) program has become a global exemplar for how a large organization can capture new opportunities for growth.

Different Sources of Growth

In this book, we'll show you why conventional approaches are often lethal to innovative growth projects and how you can supplement these approaches. Exceptional growth can be driven from three places. You can grow your core or radically improve the performance of the core by using conventional management tools. You can create new growth platforms (sometimes called adjacencies), or you can invest in strategic options that have the potential to become future platforms. As you move more and more into new platforms and strategic options, the discovery-driven tools we describe in the book become more important. Success depends on how you create an engine for growth from your capabilities and assets and properly direct it toward new spaces, using the disciplines that make sense—conventional tools if you know a lot and what we call discovery-driven tools if you don't.

Breakout growth is not only about launching bold, new initiatives. Many good growth programs begin first with incremental growth, which creates investment in learning where big new opportunities lie. That's the point at which many companies go for breakout growth. Many breakout opportunities don't look that way at first—they are the result of combining things until you finally do have a winner (Procter & Gamble's Swiffer cleaning systems would be an example). There are, of course, many companies out there making what they hope will be breakout moves. What they often find out, painfully, is that they are using the wrong tools to do it and are therefore taking on risk far beyond the potential payoff. Worse, they are learning less than they could otherwise.

In this book, we show you how your company can achieve ambitious growth targets without the hugely expensive and uncontrolled gambles that could compromise your firm. We show you the practices and disciplines that allow you to break out from the pack by an astute, disciplined, and highly aggressive strategy that massively enhances your firm's growth potential while barely increasing your risk. Discovery-driven growth principles are unique: by employing them, you can go for aggressive growth targets and *not* risk massive downside losses.

The techniques we discuss are appropriate for new growth initiatives: new ventures, new businesses, new product lines, new franchises, new locations, new markets, joint ventures, strategic alliances, and even potential mergers. The cornerstone of these disciplines is *discovery-driven planning*. Through discovery-driven planning (DDP), organizations set up bold plans to pursue futures they frame, to learn where their true futures lie, and to test their assumptions about those futures at the lowest possible cost. With DDP comes a host of other practices and disciplines that we've developed, tested, and studied over the years. We're confident that if you apply them, your growth programs are likely to be less risky and more fruitful than they would be with conventional methods.

How Discovery-Driven Is Your Mindset?

The simple quiz in table 1-1 opposite can help you highlight where your attitudes may get in the way of your developing a more discovery-driven mindset. Circle the number that best reflects your perspective of which statement most closely reflects your organization's mindset at the moment.

If your average of these responses is below 4, you will need to persuade a critical mass of your leadership team to rethink the way they go after growth opportunities. If your responses fall between 4 and 5, you're on your way but could perhaps use some work and a reminder that growth is going to require different behavior than business-as-usual. If you scored above 5, congratulations, but make sure you have processes in place to avoid slipping back when times get tough.

Discovery-Driven Planning: A Time-Tested and Proven Approach, Not Just a Theory

DDP is widely recognized for its effectiveness in helping executives find their way through highly uncertain environments. The key idea behind a discovery-driven plan is that as your plan unfolds, you want to be reducing what we call the assumption-to-knowledge ratio. When the assumption-to-knowledge ratio is high, there is a huge amount of uncertainty, and one should prioritize learning fast, at the lowest possible cost. As the ratio shrinks, focus and resource prioritization become more important. Since we first wrote about the concept in 1995 in the *Harvard Business Review*, DDP has been embraced in all kinds of contexts.[4]

Unlike many (dare we say most) popular management practices that have been enthusiastically championed before there was much evidence that they actually work, DDP has been tested again and again and shown to be effective in a broad range of organizational contexts.[5] Corporate venture units have used it to design and manage strategic growth

TABLE 1-1

Simple quiz to find your openness to discovery-driven growth

Less discovery-driven	Numerical voting	More discovery-driven
Our senior team is entirely focused on quarterly numbers and making plans.	1 2 3 4 5 6 7	Our senior team gives considerable attention to developing new businesses in addition to running today's businesses.
We don't have a lot of conversations that have to do with learning.	1 2 3 4 5 6 7	People are constantly talking about what they have learned in running their businesses.
We judge people by their individual contribution.	1 2 3 4 5 6 7	We judge people in terms of sets of opportunities.
New business development is low on the senior team's agenda.	1 2 3 4 5 6 7	New business development is item 1, 2, or 3 at most important management meetings.
We are uncomfortable with high failure rates.	1 2 3 4 5 6 7	We are prepared to cope with high failure rates, as long as the cost is contained.
You get promoted around here by demonstrating that you can drive good numbers in the core business.	1 2 3 4 5 6 7	You won't get promoted around here unless you can demonstrate that you've developed new business.
There is simply no time to think about new business—I'm swamped running my "day job."	1 2 3 4 5 6 7	We have time set aside to work on new business development in addition to our normal activities.
We evaluate projects according to calendar deadlines.	1 2 3 4 5 6 7	We evaluate projects according to key checkpoints.
We struggle with extracting any benefits from failed projects.	1 2 3 4 5 6 7	We have in place good processes that make sure we get as much as we can from a failed project.
We fund new opportunities pretty much the way we allocate funds to established businesses.	1 2 3 4 5 6 7	When it's a new opportunity, we use as few resources as possible until the idea is demonstrated.

projects. Entrepreneurs have used it to get started and communicate to investors. Venture capitalists have used it to assess the viability of potential investments. Firms have used it to assemble an overall growth program. Even not-for-profit organizations have adopted the approach. One of our favorites was a minister who used it to plan a growth strategy for his church, when he was considering different levels of personal time investment he could make in "congregation-building" activities.

The concept is taught in the curricula of leading business schools such as Wharton, Columbia, Dartmouth, Insead, Waseda, Harvard, and Northwestern (and many others) and in entrepreneurship programs at places like Stanford and Babson College. Consulting firms such as Clayton Christensen's Innosight and others have employed the technique with their clients. Our international affiliates have been using it in Germany, Switzerland, Japan, and South Korea, and we're proud to note that it has been cited in many books and articles.[6] Our point is that DDP is not armchair theorizing or an unproven management concept. Real leaders in real firms have demonstrated success with the technique, and there's no reason that you can't do likewise.

The Difference Between Conventional and Discovery-Driven Growth

All competitive advantages are subject to erosion in the face of competitive entry and changing customer requirements.[7] This implies that you have two basic choices to make: can you continue to grow by investing in an extension of competitive advantage in your core business? Or do you need to supplement this growth by creating powerful positions from new initiatives? Companies operating with a discovery-driven discipline realize sooner that their core positions are facing the threat of erosion. These firms are often much quicker and better at finding new and adjacent spaces that can be drivers of future growth. But they also are realistic about the differences between pursuing the conventional business and the disciplines that are appropriate for the new businesses.

DDG involves the systematic investment of time and effort into creating breakthrough growth in a pragmatic, low-risk way. The essential discipline is to specify a future that is both attractive and realistic and then to work backward into what has to be done today, the next day, the next week, and the next month to realize that future. The emphasis is on creating a future strategy, not driving your strategy from your past successes. Unlike conventional management practices, a discovery-driven approach begins with the assumption that you don't have the answers.

Several processes help executives plan their firms' growth and represent the first steps in DDP.

Take advantage of organizational processes. Although you want to reduce the assumption-to-knowledge ratio, DDP works best when supported by other organizational processes, as IBM found in its analysis of why emerging business opportunities were mismanaged.

Manage the growth agenda. One important practice of DDP is to consistently manage the growth agenda—and we mean that literally. A sure way to tell whether a company is serious about its growth aspirations is to see how its senior leaders allocate their own time and attention. If growth is an important goal for you, we will be looking for you to have it in the number one, two, or three position on the agenda at every significant management meeting and for the subject to be well represented in people's calendars.

Maintain high tolerance of experimentation and disappointments. Another practice involves how failures are dealt with and how success is determined. Not surprisingly, having a failure-intolerant culture in which quarterly results and immediate financial returns matter the most suppresses the generation of new ideas. Forcing those ideas that do manage to surface to conform to financial projections, such as discounted cash flow or net-present-value hurdles, distorts learning opportunities and creates inappropriate incentives (a point also made by Clayton Christensen and his colleagues).[8] Failing to balance tomorrow's opportunities with today's requirements in resource allocation usually shortchanges the future.[9]

Develop appropriate measurement and reward systems. Organizations that are good at breakthrough growth tend to use different reward and measurement practices than do companies that aren't.[10] As one of the attendees of a management seminar we ran put it: "Whenever you see someone doing something really stupid in business, there's a good chance that he thinks he's being rewarded for it." It borders on the tragic to see companies declare that they want growth, but reward their people for quarterly performance and immediate profits. Instead, consider developing measures and rewards that make sense in a high-uncertainty situation. Some guidelines:

- Create common stakes. People whose main focus is in the new opportunity area should stand to benefit from success in the core business areas; likewise, people in the core should gain from success in the new opportunities. This creates mutual shared interests.

- Don't promote people who have no exposure to growth projects. Your new business areas should rotate people through every so often. Likewise, people should not get a significant promotion without demonstrating some capability in the growth area. Your best and brightest should be clamoring to work on growth initiatives, not avoiding them.

- Set a corporate standard for growth metrics and push them to the operating level. At Procter & Gamble, for instance, CEO A. G. Lafley wanted to open the company to external innovation and started to measure what percentage of the ideas in his product groups came from outside. With a very clear goal of 50 percent at the corporate level, he had a way to measure and reward the effectiveness with which his leaders pursued the goal.

- Reward effective learning, rather than task completion. As one of our clients observed: "If I set a goal that someone's critical task for this year is to complete an acquisition, that would just be stupid. Instead, I should set the goal as doing due diligence and figuring out if the acquisition makes sense." By making learning part of what is regarded as a critical task, this leader rewarded the right behaviors.

- Create time for people to think about opportunities. Sometimes, the best innovations come from people with a little free time to tinker. 3M and Google allow people the free time to pursue their own interests. Since innovation seldom happens when your mind is occupied with the crisis of the moment, such opportunities to take a break can offer hugely valuable thinking time.

Table 1-2 summarizes the differences between conventional approaches to growth and the discovery-driven approach.

TABLE 1-2

Conventional versus discovery-driven growth

	Conventional	Discovery-driven
Success	Means making your numbers and hitting projections	Means learning as much as you can for the least possible cost
Management focus	Day-to-day and operational	Top of agenda; top of mind
Timing	Dictated by the budget or planning cycle	Dictated by key learning checkpoints
Revision	Indicates a mistake	Indicates learning
Project redirection	Seen as negative; seldom done	Seen as necessary; can be frequent
Funding	Often allocated all at once or not linked to milestone accomplishment	Limited to the amount needed to achieve next milestone; no guarantee of continuation
Assumptions	Sometimes listed; seldom checked; checking seldom integrated to whole plan	Often listed; checked frequently as part of planning process; forced integration to whole plan
Downside	Seldom explicitly managed	Acknowledged and managed before you even start
Termination decision	Delayed, avoided, and reluctantly pursued	Occurs as part of the planning process; disciplined disengagement

A Deliberately Simple Illustration of the Discovery-Driven Approach

There is no better way to understand the principles behind DDG than by an illustration. While we have used the discovery-driven approach for truly complex organizational initiatives, we find that a good way to start understanding it is to see it applied to a straightforward entrepreneurial business. This way, you can get to the essence of the technique (working backward from desired outcomes, planning to learn as you go, benchmarking against key exemplars, and the like) without excessive complexity.

So, to show the power of using discovery-driven thinking, we are going to illustrate the approach with a deliberately simple example of a start-up. As we said, don't be put off by our example's simplicity—we have used the approach to plan projects as complex as the decision to enter the Chinese market, the decision to launch an entirely new biochemical platform from a basic chemical firm, and the decision to enter into a global joint venture, among others. This example gets you into the heart of the technique without burying you in mind-numbing complexity.

A Toy Story

In May 2006, we were asked by a reporter (Jon Ortiz of the *Sacramento Bee*) what we thought of a new "experimental" toy store that was opening downtown. The owner's concept sounded like fun—it would be a place that sold old-fashioned toys, like model trains and board games. The owner would encourage shoppers to visit and experience the toys, getting kids away from the electronic distractions and back to the kind of playful experiences many of us remember from our younger days. Moreover, the shop would be located near a famous railroad museum that drew thousands of visitors monthly from all over the world, and the owner was going to copromote the shop with the partnership of the museum (he hoped). Sounds like a great concept, no?

Well, we had concerns about the idea. For one thing, the store would have to buck a lot of trends to succeed. Kids are growing out of toys earlier and earlier. They also have less free time for play than they used to (according to a University of Michigan study), since they are now involved in organized extracurricular activities such as sports. Moreover, the time kids do have is often spent with digital devices (a segment of the toy business that was worth $600 million in the United States in 2005, according to researcher NPD).[11] Wal-Mart and its peers have pushed Kay-Bee, FAO Schwartz, and Zany Brainy out of business in the last few years.

According to Ortiz, however, Troy Carlsen, our entrepreneur, was unfazed by our initial reaction. Instead, Carlsen suggested that the uniqueness of the toys and the tie-in to the railroad museum would set the shop apart from the big-box stores and give customers such a great time that Carlsen's "experiential" approach was sure to succeed.[12]

Enter discovery-driven planning. Without knowing anything more about the store (not even its name), we set to develop a discovery-driven plan for it. We started off by guessing what the founder would like to make from his efforts if his shop were to succeed. For entrepreneurs, this framing challenge is pretty individual. Let's say he's looking for $250,000 profit before taxes to make the whole thing worthwhile. If his return on sales (the money left after he's paid for his business expenses) is 50 percent (again an assumption), that means he needs to generate sales of around $500,000 to reach his business goal. Is that a realistic number? How can we know?

Well, let's think about toys. Toy sales tend to be highly cyclical—most sales take place in the eight weeks or so before the major holidays. If we make another assumption, namely, that the average price of a toy in the shop is around $25, that means he'll need to sell 20,000 of them (dividing $500,000 by $25). What do you think—feasible? Let's do a back-of-the-envelope analysis and see.

How many toys is a typical buyer likely pick up during a visit? Let's make another assumption—let's say it's two items. That means the owner will need to get 10,000 buyers into his store to make a purchase. If we further assume that the bulk of these purchases will take place in the eight weeks before the holidays, that means he needs to get 1,250 "buys" during each of those weeks. Now, obviously, not everybody who visits his store is going to be a buyer. So if we assume that the owner needs to generate five visits to the store to get one buyer, that means he needs to get 6,250 people into his store every week during those critical eight weeks of the holidays, or nearly 900 people every day, assuming he's open seven days a week during that time.

How big is the store? Newspaper reports state that it is 3,100 square feet. We don't know how much floor space he has, but that is starting to sound kind of unrealistic. Early warning! If the business pragmatically doesn't look as though it can deliver the success you need, it's time to rethink—before the money has been spent.

Even if he drops his profit aspirations to $100,000, he's still going to need to get 400 people into the store per day to hit the numbers, based on these assumptions. Even with lower profit and if the average price is higher, at $50 per item, he's still going to need 200 people . . . you get the idea. The business only starts to look feasible when the profit number drops to such a low point that we would honestly wonder why he'd go to the trouble of starting a business to take home less than the guys who deliver the boxes probably do. For those of you who are into this kind of thing, the simple spreadsheet that we used is available for download from our Web site, www.discoverydrivengrowth.com.

Just for fun, we also decided to see what the implications of having to sell 20,000 items were. Five minutes with a search engine and we had the beginning point of an answer. If you look at the population statistics, there are just under 62,000 kids below the age of nine reported to live in the Sacramento area.[13] What does that mean? Basically, the equivalent of 1 out of 3 Sacramento kids is going to need to get something from Carlsen's store every year if he needs to sell 20,000 items a year. One out of 6, if he needs to sell 10,000, and so forth. Or, he's going to have to count on nonlocal buyers.

As to the museum connection, it's a double-edged sword. The museum charges for admission—money that could be spent in the toy store. The museum also takes up people's time, time that could also be spent in the toy store. It's an open question, then, whether the museum connection will be good for Carlsen's business. Viewed differently, the museum can actually be competition.

So we're dubious about his chances for success, at least given these assumptions. That might sound hard-hearted, and to some extent, it is. Of course, entrepreneurs are unfailingly optimistic and likely to pick the analysis apart. The business will have a unique niche, they might say. It won't be *that* cyclical, given that with this design, the business will have theme-park appeal all year long. Or maybe the store is just the showcase for the real business, which is Internet based. We don't mind playing out these various scenarios on paper—we haven't put any money at risk (yet). All we're trying to do is to figure out whether the likely return he's going to get for the risk of starting the business is worthwhile.

Or Maybe the Model Is Wrong

On the other hand, a couple of shining examples in the toy business seem to have overcome the challenges we have just anticipated. For instance, the fantastically successful Build-A-Bear Workshop, in which kids get to assemble the toys in the store, has stores that average about 3,000 square feet as well. But unlike our model, which is based on a Toys "R" Us concept shrunk to miniature form, the Build-A-Bear Workshop model stresses the experience. Kids make the toys, choose the vital parts and names, get clothes and accessories for them, and so on. The upshot is that a typical Build-A-Bear Workshop store generates $700 per square foot, for an average of $2.1 million per store. It's a brilliant business model—you pay to supply the free labor that creates the product!

Another fascinating example from the toy business is the American Girl doll phenomenon, which has spawned American Girl Place shops. According to some pundits, a typical family visiting the American Girl Place will spend around $300 for such items as doll haircuts, an American doll review, lunch, and accessories. This is only going to be more attractive with the launch of the first American Girl movie in 2008. Our point would be that Carlsen's toy business will have to be a lot more American Girl and a lot less Toys "R" Us to work, given the size and scale of his Sacramento store.

This is the starting point for a discovery-driven way of thinking—define and frame success before you even start, and make sure that it will be worth it! If the idea doesn't hold together at this stage, don't do it—life is too full of other wonderful opportunities.

We are the last people on earth to quash anybody's dreams. The dilemma is that unless the risk is worth taking at first blush (and while you are still optimistic), the result is likely to be a costly disappointment. Well, our qualms aside, Troy Carlsen went ahead and opened the store. It's G. Willikers in Sacramento and is featured as a tourist attraction in the old town section.

As of August 2008, the store was still in business, although it seems to have been lumped together with its founders' sister business, Stage Nine Entertainment. As far as we can tell, G. Willikers has moved from a straight "toy" unit of business to an "experience" unit of business, consistent with the conclusions we reached from doing the framing part of the discovery-driven plan. A recent customer wrote a glowing review of the store, but did lodge one complaint: "My only complaint is that I bought an item and then saw the exact same item over at Evangelines for 3 bucks less. Hmmph! Oh well, I support their creative play intentions."[14]

Three Parts of Discovery-Driven Growth

What you are basically doing with DDG is investing to keep your options open for as long as possible. Like buying an option, you don't want to take on any more risk than is warranted by the information you have available to you. As an executive at one company we work with suggests: "It's a deadly discipline—unlike the fuzziness that you have when you do the 'increment sales by 10 percent each year' kind of spreadsheet, it forces you to be very specific."

Discovery-driven growth, as the name suggests, harnesses the essential discovery process required in high-uncertainty situations so that you can benefit from it. By following the principles we lay out in the book, you can become expert at three sets of activities that we have found relevant to success:

1. *Creating a focus on strategic growth:* aligning your company's strategy with resource allocations and project approvals and connecting the growth strategy with specific, actionable opportunities

2. *Executing strategic growth projects:* learning to manage actual projects that are the real core of your strategy

3. *Making discovery-driven growth work for you:* weaving DDG into the culture of your company

The three sets of activities form the three parts of this book. The rest of this chapter tells you what you'll find in its pages.

Organization of This Book

This book is organized to reflect the sequence of steps we have found to be most straightforward and practical when a firm is developing a DDG strategy. We believe that if your company is among the 65 percent whose CEOs are, according to a recent IBM-commissioned survey, planning radical changes in the next two years, these techniques can save you an enormous amount of frustration and wasted time, if not out-and-out failure.[15]

Part 1: Focusing on Strategic Growth

The first part of the book covers the strategic considerations of growth. In chapter 2, we establish the point of departure for your approach to growth by framing the challenge for the organization as a whole. This chapter considers the growth challenge at the CEO or senior team level as these executives begin to define the growth frame for the entire enterprise. The outcome of this process is a set of propositions about which initiatives will be needed to realistically create growth. As a result, everybody else in the company will be clear about what kinds of growth opportunities are legitimate, and which will therefore be supported, because they are a good strategic fit.

Chapter 3 builds on chapter 2 by first analyzing how resources are currently being allocated to growth and then considering how these allocations would need to change, given the framing work of chapter 2. We take a portfolio view of different kinds of growth opportunities. How much growth needs to come from the core business? How much from adjacencies? Will the whole portfolio deliver the growth that you need to keep your growth commitments to stakeholders?

In chapter 4, we show you how to connect your strategy and internal practices to your specific strategic initiatives. After you decide what is necessary for a corporate goal, we take up the issue of framing an initiative. We show you how to specify what success must look like in terms of upside potential before you even consider making an investment. We look at a specific strategic initiative and how you would start a discovery-driven plan for it.

Part 2: Executing Specific Growth Opportunities

Part 2 looks at strategic projects and how you manage them. In reality, your strategy is what projects you are working on and how you run them, not what's printed in the annual report or posted on your Web site. Thus, whether you are a CEO or someone else in the organizational pecking order, you must have the right practices in place to manage strategic growth initiatives effectively.

Chapter 5 has to do with designing the fundamental business that will generate the growth. You need to identify a *unit of business* that will create the architecture of your business model. A unit of business is quite literally what the customer pays for. At the same time, you'll need to think through what key measures will ultimately drive success in your business. We also suggest how you can compare your key metrics for the growth business with those of potentially competitive organizations. This is often a reality check for business planners, who make assumptions that might seem sensible in the rarefied atmosphere of a planning office, but fail the competitive reality check.

In Chapter 6, we introduce the tools that help keep a discovery-driven plan coherent and connected to reality. Among these are the reverse income statement and the reverse balance sheet. We now tie together the decisions you made in the earlier chapters and then simulate your future business in a way that allows you to make big adjustments, engage in what-if speculation, and assure yourself that you are being realistic—all while the investment in the future business is extremely small.

Chapter 7 outlines a core discipline of DDP: the documentation and testing of assumptions as you develop your operational plan. In this chapter, we show you how to develop an operational specification and an assumption checklist, how to test assumptions, and the financial logic that underlies the business model. We also show you how operational activities and assumptions are intimately linked and offer suggestions for containing risk and reducing costs as you try to test your assumptions. This chapter also discusses the critical function of the checkpoint review process. We also look here at the best practices in redirecting projects. Our research suggests that projects in companies that successfully use discovery-driven strategy frequently redirect projects, yet very little management literature describes how this works.

Chapter 8 takes on the challenge you will face when you have to shut projects down, what we call the painful but necessary art of disengagement. How do you make sure that killing an initiative is seen as a constructive process that allows the company to benefit as much as possible from the investments it has made? Here, we also discuss the all-important question of how you handle the inevitably disappointed stakeholders and supporters for the project, as well as the politics of the project-termination decision.

Part 3: Making Discovery-Driven Growth Work for You

Chapter 9 describes how other firms have implemented a discovery-driven strategy. We suggest how you can build DDG into your everyday life at work, building on the experiences of other companies that have now institutionalized the approach.

Finally, in chapter 10, we outline the elements of an ongoing growth program that we've found to be important. We move from the design of a new-business development group to the critical tasks of the CEO in making growth a real priority.

You'll see that the processes outlined in the book have implications for how you lead, plan, and manage strategic growth initiatives. As an additional help for our readers, we've created a road map that shows the entire process and where you are at any given point as you work through the book. You'll see that some of the activities we describe are relevant to corporate leadership, while others speak more to the level of an individual strategic initiative.

Let's turn now to the next chapter—a point of departure for a discovery-driven plan, the articulation of what is going to be needed to achieve the growth aspirations of the entire company.

Roadmap of the book

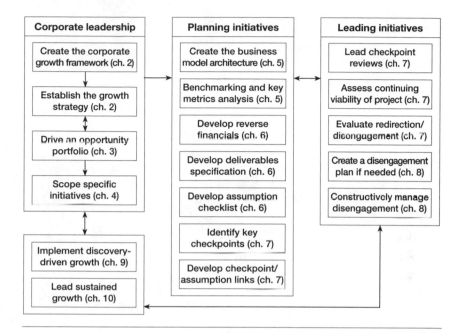

Corporate leadership	Planning initiatives	Leading initiatives
Create the corporate growth framework (ch. 2)	Create the business model architecture (ch. 5)	Lead checkpoint reviews (ch. 7)
Establish the growth strategy (ch. 2)	Benchmarking and key metrics analysis (ch. 5)	Assess continuing viability of project (ch. 7)
Drive an opportunity portfolio (ch. 3)	Develop reverse financials (ch. 6)	Evaluate redirection/ disengagement (ch. 7)
Scope specific initiatives (ch. 4)	Develop deliverables specification (ch. 6)	Create a disengagement plan if needed (ch. 8)
	Develop assumption checklist (ch. 6)	Constructively manage disengagement (ch. 8)
Implement discovery-driven growth (ch. 9)	Identify key checkpoints (ch. 7)	
Lead sustained growth (ch. 10)	Develop checkpoint/ assumption links (ch. 7)	

I

Focusing on Strategic Growth

This part of the book starts off with your corporate-level strategy. In our experience, one of the major obstacles to a successful growth program is the lack of clarity about the overall strategy in the first place. We can't tell you the number of times we've seen well-intentioned project managers waste their time and energy on initiatives that senior managers felt were not "on strategy," often after the initiatives had been approved by those very same senior managers. Similarly, we've seen a lot of good companies waste enormous amounts of resources on too many projects that had too little focus. So in the next three chapters, you'll be thinking about the big picture—growth at the level of the company, how that translates into specific resource allocations, and then how that breaks into discovery-driven frames at the level of individual strategic initiatives.

CHAPTER TWO

Creating Your
Growth Framework

This chapter is oriented toward the role of senior executives in establishing clear, focused guidelines for the pursuit of growth. By definition, these guidelines also help people understand where they should not waste their time. Providing a strategic framework for your business requires that the senior team in your company (or senior leadership at a divisional level, if that is where strategic planning takes place) establish the boundaries for success at the outset. In a sensible planning horizon (typically three to seven years, depending on the competitive pace of your industry), how much growth in revenues or, even better, in profits would constitute a successful outcome? It's important to be crystal clear on this, as it drives the rest of your strategy. Next, the senior team's job is to develop a set of propositions about what contribution the various initiatives will make to future growth. Where will

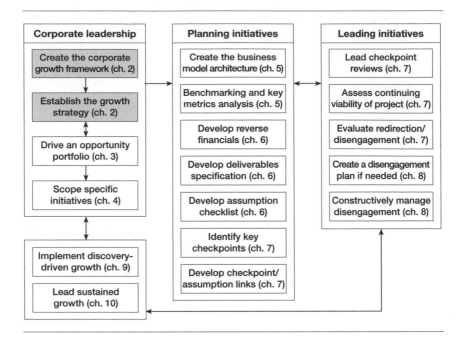

Corporate leadership	Planning initiatives	Leading initiatives
Create the corporate growth framework (ch. 2)	Create the business model architecture (ch. 5)	Lead checkpoint reviews (ch. 7)
Establish the growth strategy (ch. 2)	Benchmarking and key metrics analysis (ch. 5)	Assess continuing viability of project (ch. 7)
Drive an opportunity portfolio (ch. 3)	Develop reverse financials (ch. 6)	Evaluate redirection/ disengagement (ch. 7)
Scope specific initiatives (ch. 4)	Develop deliverables specification (ch. 6)	Create a disengagement plan if needed (ch. 8)
	Develop assumption checklist (ch. 6)	Constructively manage disengagement (ch. 8)
Implement discovery-driven growth (ch. 9)	Identify key checkpoints (ch. 7)	
Lead sustained growth (ch. 10)	Develop checkpoint/ assumption links (ch. 7)	

future profits come from, and through which kinds of initiatives? Which areas will be expected to grow new sales? Which areas should be cut back? Which should drive efficiency gains? Which should penetrate new markets? Which should leverage new technologies? Which should leverage acquisitions? The goal is not necessarily to be right; rather, it is to provide some sense of coherence around which the rest of the strategy can be aligned.

The aspects of the process this chapter touches on—highlighted with shading in our road map above—have to do with creating the growth framework and establishing the growth strategy.

Specify Success First

As an example, consider how Mark Hurd framed the challenges for Hewlett Packard when he first moved into the CEO's office in 2005:

One of his first moves after arriving at HP was to work with his team to set the financial targets they think the company should hit by 2008. From there, he and his lieutenants worked backwards and laid out the metrics for each segment of the company. Those calculations helped them arrive at the 14,500 [worker] layoff figure and determine that HP can sustain the $3.5 billion-a-year R&D budget they want. With a specific goal three years out, "you can start thinking about the future with a little less emotion and a little more analytics," [Hurd] says.[1]

Between October 2005 and October 2007, HP grew its revenues from $86.7 million to $104.3 billion, an impressive gain for a company in the hypercompetitive electronics markets. Even more impressive is that the company was able to operate more efficiently, reducing selling and general administrative costs without harming revenue growth. The combined effect of Hurd's strategy was to increase net income from $2.4 billion to $7.3 billion between 2005 and 2007.[2] Of course, in dynamic markets, no success lasts forever, and by the time you read this, HP too may have stumbled. But from 2005 to 2008, the company was widely regarded as being on the right track and Hurd's approach certainly seemed to have played a major role.

Such reverse thinking helped establish the original goals and created a company norm of pursuing them with a little less emotion and a little more analytics. What you are looking for in your own company is a good frame that is clear, easy to understand and to communicate, and actionable. A good frame provides the foundation for discovery-driven growth by outlining what you want to accomplish.

One of the main purposes of establishing a clear frame at the top is that it helps the senior team clearly articulate what kinds of opportunities are likely to be worthwhile and, equally important, which kinds will *not* be worthwhile. A clear frame reinforces the point that business-as-usual is unlikely to lead to breakthrough growth. Left to their own devices, employees of most companies will come up with incremental,

of strategic intent: Edward S. Jones aims to "grow to 17,000 financial advisers by 2012 (from about 10,000 today) by offering trusted and convenient face-to-face financial advice to conservative individual investors who delegate their financial decisions, through a national network of one-financial-adviser offices." The statement specifies success in terms of a growth goal, then lays out how the firm is expected to meet the goal. While this statement leaves a lot of scope for action, there are also many alternatives that are prohibited under it. For instance, Edward S. Jones would rule out Internet-based advising or having clients bent on speculative growth.

The question of strategic focus is directly connected to the core capabilities that give firms a competitive advantage. Absent clear guidance with respect to what capabilities should be built up and which should be abandoned, the result is often random drift and squandered resources. This is particularly important if the growth strategy is changed, because if it isn't clearly communicated to the people who actually deploy resources and make decisions, capabilities will continue to be built up around the old strategy, which again is a waste of resources. Finally, strategies also need to be fairly persistent over time, unless external forces disrupt the strategy. If they change too frequently, the buildup of capabilities is interrupted and a critical mass of capability in any given area of focus cannot develop.[6]

Focusing on Attractive Markets
Where Your Capabilities Count

Texas Instruments is exemplary in how its senior leaders conceived and executed against a dramatic change of focus for the company, then communicated it clearly to key stakeholders, such as shareholders and customers. *Chief Executive* magazine summarized the strategic shift: "Within two years, he [Thomas Engibous, TI's CEO] had sold off nearly all divisions unrelated to digital signal processors and analog chips, which convert sensory information such as images and sounds into the digital language of computers."[7] TI spun off businesses that were not within this strategic framework, including its automotive, heating, ventilating, and air-conditioning operations, which were sold to Bain Capital, and its defense-related businesses, which were sold to Raytheon.

George Consolver, currently the director of TI's strategy process, recalled the change in an interview with us: "If you roll the clock back to 1996, 1997, 1998 . . . we really focused in on our semiconductor business. The early stages of that had to do with the transition into something that at the time we labeled the 'networked society.' We wanted to get in on growth in the early stages of Internet activity as well as cellular communications."

Essentially, senior leadership at TI created a framework for what the company was going to do and not do; the framework was different from what it had used in the past. As Consolver told us, the three areas that were considered to be in the strategic frame were semiconductors, digital signal processing, and digital light processing. At the time of our conversation (February 27, 2006), he attributed $10 billion to $12 billion in additional growth that these businesses were able to drive. The results of a clear refocusing at TI have been remarkable. Figure 2-1 shows the stock performance of the company over a long period. Note the sharp uptick in market value after the 1996 refocusing decisions. This did not just happen; senior leadership chose where the company was going to compete as well as where it would *not* compete.

Getting the Senior Team on Board Early

Having a clear focus that is agreed to by senior-level executives became a core thrust of a major program at DuPont. The program, which we were involved with for many years, was called the Knowledge-Intensive University (KIU) program. It began in 1999, as Chad Holliday, DuPont's

FIGURE 2-1

Stock price performance of Texas Instruments, 1980 to present

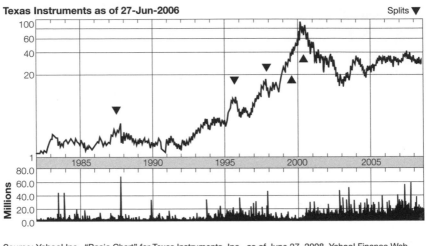

Texas Instruments as of 27-Jun-2006

Source: Yahoo! Inc., "Basic Chart" for Texas Instruments, Inc., as of June 27, 2008, Yahoo! Finance Web page, http://finance.yahoo.com/q/bc?s=TXN&t=my&l=on&z=m&q=l&c=. Reproduced with permission of Yahoo! Inc. ® 2008 by YAHOO! Inc. YAHOO! and the YAHOO! logo are trademarks of Yahoo! Inc.

CEO, sought to shift the direction of the company from pure product innovation to a focus on "getting paid for what we know." This was in contrast to DuPont's traditional business model, in which consulting and services were given away to promote product utilization.[8]

Holliday's articulation of building greater knowledge intensity at the corporate level is similar to other senior-level guidelines that seek to shift a company's center of gravity. At IBM, for instance, the mantra of on-demand computing set the stage for Big Blue's current thrust in software and services, transforming the company into a solutions business rather than a hardware-focused one. At P&G, A. G. Lafley's insistence that 50 percent of innovations come from outside the company, coupled with the goals of growing its big brands, created the high-level framework. Within those broad, higher-level objectives, however, individual business leaders need to specify what kinds of growth initiatives would address the challenge.[9]

In DuPont, this was a lesson learned through frustrating experience. With Holliday's support, the KIU team, under the direction of Bob Cooper, set out to create a "companywide culture that celebrates growth" after many years of focusing on efficiency (in part 3 of the book, we'll look at the general principles for getting started with a growth program such as this).[10] The team members started off by creating workshops to identify opportunities and did indeed get some initiatives going on a small scale. That's when they came up against a major gap—while division leaders understood the broad objectives of the growth program, they had not yet reached alignment on the definition of success or the competitive arenas in which the company hoped to win. As a consequence, resources for growth initiatives were inconsistently allocated or not allocated at all, growth was not part of people's performance evaluations, and most of the projects stalled, just as occurred at IBM before the adoption of the EBO program. As Cooper later put it: "We started in April of '99 naively thinking all we needed was to bring a group of smart people together from a given business, create a stimulating environment to generate ideas, and growth would happen."[11]

Senior leaders, absent a chance to rethink how they frame the business, are understandably focused on the issues of the here and now. This has been identified as a major barrier to growth in many studies.[12] What's needed is to shift the agenda of the senior team away from today's business and toward the business of the future.

At DuPont, the solution was to involve the leadership teams for growth arenas from the start, forcing them to achieve alignment on what success would look like and what arenas to pursue before specific opportunities were launched. The design of the KIU interventions was subsequently changed to incorporate a half- to full-day leadership session at both the front end and the back end of the business definition process. The outputs of the front-end session included the articulation of a core mission, a number of screening statements that would specify what variables make an opportunity more or less attractive, the specification of permissible growth domains, a commitment to provide time and resources by the senior leadership, a short communication (which we called an elevator speech), and the initiation of necessary organizational changes to support the growth initiatives. The back-end leadership session scored proposals against the screening criteria and led the team to commit to funding resources for approved initiatives.[13]

Outputs of a Typical Leadership Framing Session

The KIU team eventually settled on a few core outputs that we found helped create alignment and strategic clarity among the senior team.

Core mission. DuPont calls the core mission the articulation of the core customer value to be enhanced by deploying a DuPont capability. In DuPont's decorative-surfaces business, for instance, the team eventually decided to move from providing product and material functionality as the key driver of success to creating what Cooper called a "wow" for customers with its Zodiac brand, which had been designed to compete with granite in high-end home applications. This exercise fundamentally changed the company's direction and today, sales are booming. The core mission served as an aligned, strategic direction for the business.[14]

Screening statements. Screening statements make it crystal clear which opportunities are desirable and which aren't and allow ideas to be mapped against the same set of criteria. In the case of KIU, common screening elements included the market attractiveness, the ease of commercialization, and the uniqueness or defensibility of the offer. We helped DuPont get to these common elements by retrospectively examining past initiatives and defining the elements that tended to accelerate or inhibit success. We then worked with the leadership team to develop specific scoring elements for each statement. The scores are deliberately somewhat skewed. Table 2-1 provides an example of one of the templates in use at DuPont.

TABLE 2-1

Partial screening scorecard template for market relevance at DuPont

Dimension	Exceptional if . . . (top score of 9)	Acceptable if . . . (score of 5)	Unfavorable or "a problem" if . . . (score of 1 or less)
Strong customer pull	There is clear evidence either from needs-based segmentation or actual customer experimentation that customer demand is strong.	There is evidence the customer desires our offering through discussions—we asked what the customer wants from DuPont as an example.	Customer demand was determined by internal studies.
Favorable trends	There are very strong macroeconomic, industry, or regulatory trends that favor our offering to the customer.	The trends appear to be neutral to our offering.	The market seems to be working against us.
Size of DuPont opportunity	The potential size of the opportunity in 3–5 years is $500 million or more.	The potential size of the opportunity in 3–5 years is $100–$499 million.	The potential size of the opportunity in 3–5 years is under $100 million.
Ability to create a discontinuity	Our offering has the potential to fundamentally change how our customers do business.	Our offering significantly improves how our customers do business.	Our offering meets the physical attributes our customers request.
Route-to-market position	We can secure a very strong, defensible route to market.	We can get to market.	Our route to market will most likely be blocked without significant effort to restructure the industry.

It takes real commitment on the part of the leadership team to work through such statements in the table in detail, but in our experience, it's time worth taking. Having rich discussions about which elements of a project really matter can create enormous clarity among the team and promote alignment. Moreover, there is no one best set of screening statements—the things that would make a project appealing to one company might cause it to be rejected at another.

Potential growth domains. Like the aforementioned clear strategic statement put forth by Edward S. Jones, the DuPont leaders lay out potential growth domains. That is, they define which customers the company seeks to serve, how it will create value, and what the source of competitive differentiation will be. Cooper describes how this worked for another DuPont business area:

> A good example to bring these concepts alive is our work with the Safety and Protection (S&P) growth platform lead by Ellen Kullman, Group VP. The businesses had previously been defined by what products they sold (Kevlar, for example). In the leadership session at the KIU, it was determined that the Safety and Protection platform would pursue businesses which contributed to the safety and/or protection of people or things, often coming up with solutions rather than product offers.[15]

> The Safety and Protection area, according to a 2008 press release, has enjoyed 65 percent growth since its assembly in 2002 as part of the KIU process and is poised to enjoy continued vigorous growth globally.[16]

In addition to the preceding tasks, leaders at the session were asked to make specific resource commitments, including funding a business-building process and freeing leaders from other commitments in order to create focus on growth. The leaders were also asked to prepare a short communication (short enough that it could be delivered in one elevator trip!) to make sure that they could pare away the irrelevant or unnecessary elements from their message. The managers further committed to making the necessary organizational and structural changes to promote the growth ventures (actually using the kite framework from our *MarketBusters* book).[17]

The KIU project at DuPont is still very much embedded with the way the company pursues growth opportunities. According to Dan Edgar, who has inherited many of the KIU processes from Cooper (who has since retired), the process is most recently in active use as the company pursues opportunities in emerging markets. Indeed, DuPont's emerging-market strategy has been widely praised as a source of major growth for the firm and a bright spot for investors.[18]

Details of Actual Framing Sessions

The executives at DuPont learned that without a clear leadership frame, well-intentioned efforts to grow suffer from a lack of strategic focus. Since we benefited from the lessons learned in that program, let's look at a company we worked with, in which the recognition of the senior team's role in developing a clear frame was already in place.

The essence of discovery-driven growth is that a company specifies the strategic outcome it desires and then learns its way into its unfolding future. Specifically, once the goals are framed at the corporate level, a suite of initiatives and their associated projects must then be planned, each of which focuses on specific drivers of growth or productivity improvement. Each major initiative gets its own plan. In this chapter, we are looking at the framing exercise; in chapter 3, we will look at how the suite of growth initiatives is generated.

Ingredients, Inc.: Driving a Growth Agenda

The following paragraphs describe the detailed activities of an actual corporate-level framing session. It was a project for a subsidiary firm of a large European-based multinational that had been put together largely through acquisitions. The firm researches, locates, and manufactures ingredients that are used by other companies in their end products, so let's call the company Ingredients, Inc. The CEO, who had a strong growth mandate from corporate to drive organic growth and profitability improvement, engaged us to help drive his growth agenda. The engagement lasted for about nine months and incorporated both executive-level decision-making meetings as well as opportunity brainstorming and project-specific DDP sessions. The goal was to launch the company on an innovation-based growth program after the years it had spent integrating and consolidating operations.

The first meeting, which took place in January 2006, consisted of basically sharing insights about the business with the executive team, some subject-matter experts, and ourselves. About a month later, we suggested that the firm gather the entire decision-making executive team, a few knowledgeable nonexecutive subject-matter experts, and us and hold an all-day session to establish the corporatewide frame, before getting into the opportunity search or DDP exercises. We explained the concept of *framing* for the growth program and asked the group to discuss what would really make the investment of time and effort worthwhile. For this discussion, we told the participants, they needed to consider where they wanted to be in the future.

The CEO noted that when he had taken the job, Ingredients, Inc., was the eighth-ranked player in its arena by revenues and that his clear mandate was to move the company into the top five within three years, with the goal of getting it to the top three within five years. This is very often the impetus for defining a growth goal. It might be a benchmark against key rivals, the expectations of shareholders for certain returns, or an aspiration to achieve critical mass in an industry. Absent an alternative, we like to benchmark against competition (or organizations that are admired by our clients) to start considering realistic targets. We'll give a specific example of how this works in chapter 4.

For Ingredients, Inc., the aiming point was to improve its standing within its industry segment. With this established, we then worked through what it would mean for the company financially to aspire to this position, what growth could be expected from the underlying base business, and what growth would have to be generated by new businesses. The team's best guess was that in a three-year horizon, the base business would grow by about 12 percent, at profits of about 15 percent, which left a considerable gap that would have to be filled by new businesses. Among the team's conclusions was that the existing methods for finding such opportunities weren't going to be able to meet this kind of growth target (just as Jeff Bezos of Amazon.com noted: left to business-as-usual, people tend to come up with incremental ideas). Without knowing exactly what new ideas we would then turn up in the rest of the process, the team specified that its new strategy should be to have five to ten specific growth opportunities with a target revenue number and the capacity to drive a 15 percent profit margin or better.

While the team seemed a little daunted at first, we suggested that this discussion simply brought to light (early, before any money had been spent) some critically important framing issues. First, growth goals were unlikely to be met in a five-year time frame by organic growth alone—acquisitions were going to continue to be important. Second, incremental improvement was unlikely to deliver the required growth—truly breakthrough opportunities were going to be needed. Third, the search for opportunities would have to go beyond current industry solutions, since the best businesses in the industry as currently configured could not meet a growth challenge of this magnitude. Finally, progress made on the operational excellence and efficiency frontiers would need to be continued if the profitability of the enterprise was to be improved on an ongoing basis.

We wrapped up the meeting with a clear definition of the kinds of projects that would potentially fit this frame in terms of fit with the company, ability to drive growth, and utilization of capabilities. The senior team itself participated in developing the initial set of screening statements and tested them against some proposals that were currently under way. This created a tremendous sense of alignment and focus. We also kept it cheap—with the exception of the costs to organize the meeting, virtually no money was spent exploring ideas that would fail to meet the frame or would fail the screens. In this case, deciding what *not* to do conserved scarce resources from the very start.

growth, margins, and return on assets (ROA), for ESCO and for best-of-breed (in other words, high-performing) companies in its industry. Table 2-2 shows the ESCO situation in 2006.

As you can see, the 2006 profits of $95 million were the result of several years of modest performance at best. For five years, sales growth had been less than 2 percent annually, margins were slim and declining, and ROA was low. In addition, the competitive market was fierce and other companies were outperforming ESCO on most of the key dimensions. This can be seen by the right-most column, which shows the five-year growth performance of what the CEO called the best-of-breed competitor. Though the top competitor was not exactly posting Google-like results, ESCO was nevertheless being outperformed on every dimension. To get Google-like results is impractical in an industry like this, unless there is some huge technology breakthrough that can be deployed.

With respect to the targets for growth themselves (the first step in a discovery-driven strategy), the new CEO suggested (with the support of the senior team) that his company should seek to outperform its best-of-breed competitor in profit terms. Without entering into fantasy-land (given the tough industry structure that distribution is in), the CEO and his colleagues thought that a reasonable growth aspiration for the 2007–2012 period would be a profit growth target of 6 per-

TABLE 2-2

ESCO performance data

| | 2006 | 2001 | FIVE-YEAR TREND IN ANNUAL GROWTH | |
			ESCO	Best of breed
Profits	$95 million	$88 million	1.59%	
Sales	$1.9 billion	$1.7 billion		
Sales growth	4.7%	4.6%	0.43%	6.0%
ROS	5.0%	5.3%	−1.13%	5.5%
ROA	8.0%	7.9%	0.3%	8.5%

ROS, return on sales; ROA, return on assets.

cent, compounded for the next five years, with accompanying increases in both ROA and return on sales (ROS). This became the frame for the growth program to be designed. It also illuminated the significant challenge the team would have in meeting that goal, as you can see from the "Difference" column in table 2-3. This column essentially says that ESCO will have to figure out a way to generate $33 million more in profits from the growth program than it generates today.

One can further define the challenge by showing what the aspired profit target implies for other elements of the business. Table 2-4 shows the performance challenges, which proved considerable. The combination of increased profits and profitability called for an increase in profits of 35 percent, but to meet the growth in profitability targets, this increase of 35 percent had to be accompanied by more efficient performance on three dimensions: sales needed to be increased by 22.7 percent, costs could not grow by more than 22.1 percent, and assets could only be increased by 8 percent. Although the numbers looked daunting, they were sufficiently specific that one could decide whether a given idea was likely to overcome the hurdles or not. This is a huge benefit of DDP: it makes assumptions and relationships between business elements explicit so that they can be tested.

This analysis illustrates the growth-framing principles of setting forth the corporate-level strategic goals. In the next chapter we will revisit the issue of deciding which projects and other activities will be needed to meet them.

TABLE 2-3

Creating a worthwhile frame at ESCO

	Expected increment	2006	2012 target	Difference
Profits	35%	$95 million	$128.3 million	$33.3 million
ROA		8%	10.0%	
ROS		5%	5.5%	

ROA, return on assets; ROS, return on sales.

TABLE 2-4

Implications of the profit growth challenge for ESCO

	2006	2012	Increase	Percent increase
Required profits	$95 million	$128.3 million	$33.3 million	35.0%
Required revenues	$1.9 billion	$2.3 billion	$431.8 million	22.7%
Allowable costs	$1.8 billion	$2.2 billion	$398.6 million	22.1%
Allowable assets	$1.2 billion	$1.3 billion	$95 million	8.0%

ACTION STEPS

Let's wrap up this chapter by summarizing the action steps. These apply to the executive team that will be setting the specific growth strategies for a division or business, within the broad approach outlined at the senior level of the company (the two groups might be the same, but are often different). Thus, the planning teams within DuPont operated at the business or growth-platform level, but under the guidance of the knowledge-intensive mandate.

1. Working as a team, agree on challenging but realistic new standards of performance that you think will push your company to the edge of its capabilities, but not over the edge. Set standards for increased revenues and increased profitability. What would success look like?

2. Now, working backward, analyze your existing portfolio to determine whether there is enough in your pipeline of initiatives to deliver the levels of performance required by your new frame. If not, try to specify the number and type of new initiatives (both efficiency oriented and growth oriented) that would roughly get you to the right performance level.

3. Specify, as best you can, what core value you think you bring to customers and the domains (geographic, technological, and so

46

on) that you'd like to participate in. Try to make these statements fairly specific, so that it is clear what kinds of projects will be in, or desirable, and which will be out, or undesirable.

4. Agree as a team on a set of screening statements that you can commit to using. Test the screens on a few of your proposed initiatives and then refine them. You'll be using the screens to make some important portfolio decisions in the next part of the process, so it makes sense to take this exercise extremely seriously.

CHAPTER THREE

Aligning the Organization for Growth

This chapter assumes that you've taken the first step toward creating a plan for discovery-driven growth, namely, specifying a clear and unambiguous growth strategy on the part of senior leadership, with a concrete set of screening statements that are a guide to which opportunities are worth pursuing and which are not. Achieving real growth, however, requires more than a specification of a compelling frame—it needs resource allocation and focused attention. So in this chapter, we'll review how you can make sure that your resources and other organizational capabilities are being aligned with what your senior team has articulated as the strategy.

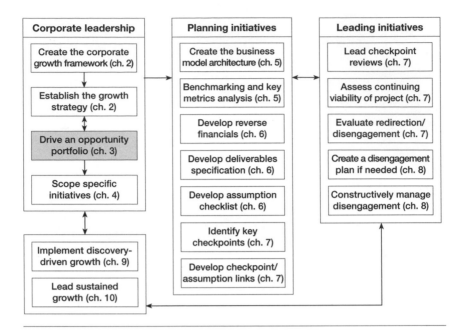

Among the decisions you'll be wrestling with at this stage are whether you should make investments in highly uncertain projects that might have a big payoff or whether you should stick to projects with a more likely rate of success but which are less likely to be major hits. Should you be emphasizing the core business, or should you be focusing attention further afield? And what about appropriately rewarding and leading the people who will be managing the growth programs? We find that a helpful next step is to get a conceptual map of where resources are being allocated in your company right now. Then, you can begin to see if the pattern of resource allocation to initiatives is likely to support your strategy. After all, your allocation of resources to programs and initiatives *is* your strategy, whatever your strategy Power-Point deck says. We'll start with a concept we call the opportunity portfolio. This part of the process is shaded in the road map of the book shown above.

Your Growth Landscape: The Opportunity Portfolio

To connect the broad frame at the top of the organization to specific growth initiatives, it's important that the senior team (and each relevant general management team working with it at business or divisional levels) have a clear picture of what the company is spending its resources on. The senior team also needs a process for making sure that resource allocations and strategy are aligned. One of the most popular tools we've developed to do this is an opportunity portfolio map, which we introduced in our first book and have subsequently enhanced.[1] An *opportunity portfolio* is a visual map of the major initiatives going on in your organization. It brings together in one place the critical information that allows the senior team to see whether the frames it has established are effectively aligned and effectively resourced.

An opportunity portfolio, as pictured in figure 3-1, looks at initiatives in the context of the amount of uncertainty the firm is facing for each initiative. Across the bottom, we have market and organizational uncertainty. Where such uncertainty is high, you may not know who the customers are, what price they will be prepared to pay, how to distribute the offer, or what its key selling points are. Where it's low, you should have a pretty good idea of these variables. Along the vertical side is what we call technical, or capability, uncertainty. Where this is high, you may not know what the technical standards are, whether the execution challenges can be met at the right cost, what skills are going to be important, whether you can get enough of them, and so on. Obviously, the more a particular project falls into the upper right-hand side of the figure, the greater the level of uncertainty you have and the more unpredictable an initiative is likely to be. Discovery-driven-growth tools, such as discovery-driven planning, become more useful as you move to the upper right-hand edge of the figure. Conventional tools and plans remain useful when you are working in the southwest corners of the figure.

FIGURE 3-1

An opportunity portfolio

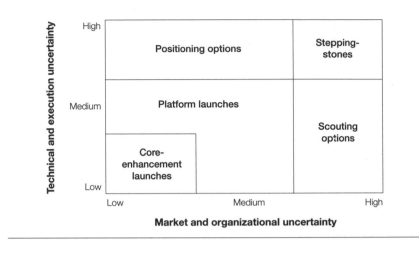

There are many ways to portray a particular portfolio. We started off by picturing each major initiative as a bubble, with person-months to completion as a number in the bubble, and bubble size representing its upside potential. With this depiction, we could easily get an idea of whether the investment (in terms of people's time) and the payoff were consistent, as well as appropriate to the level of uncertainty we were working with. In the years since we introduced that simple concept, companies have adapted many variations. Color-coding to reflect linkages of projects to specific strategic initiatives is common, as is incorporating additional information with the use of broken or solid lines, types of fill, different shapes—really, there is no hard and fast rule about how a chart can be put together. The only rule is this—however you decide to do it, be consistent from project to project; try to make sure that the judgments about what falls where are seen as transparent and fair.

Each of the areas in the growth portfolio reflects initiatives with somewhat different management implications. The different types of growth opportunities have different roles in a portfolio, but all of them are important. The portfolio can help you choose when to use conventional tools (such as discounted cash-flow analysis) and when to use discovery-driven growth tools (such as discovery-driven planning, which we'll cover in subsequent chapters).

Core-Enhancement Launches

Core-enhancement launches are projects that improve the profit streams and growth of the core business. Although these launches may be highly innovative, they are building upon or enhancing a business with which your firm is already successful. Investments in improving operational effectiveness fall into this category, as do upgrades to major systems such as the information technology (IT), human resources (HR), or supply-chain systems. The operational-effectiveness projects are aimed at improving the profitability of current revenues and are often a key part of a company's growth strategy. Indeed, without such initiatives, it is very hard to sustain a lead against motivated competitors.

Although Apple has always been known for highly innovative and stylish products, a key underpinning for its turnaround after founder Steve Jobs returned to the company in 1996 was a renewed focus on efficiency and operations. As a shocked *BusinessWeek* reporter noted in a 2000 cover story:

> Get a load of this: The company known for its incorrigible, free-spirited, free-spending ways has become a master of operating efficiencies. Jobs has slashed expenses from $8.1 billion in 1997 to $5.7 billion in 1999 by outsourcing manufacturing, trimming inventories, shifting 25% of sales to an online store, and slicing the number of distributors from the double digits to two. That, combined with the new products, has won back allies.[2]

Other types of core-enhancement projects seek to enhance their revenue streams by growing into new markets, penetrating existing customers' wallets more deeply, or extending existing brands into adjacent areas. Procter & Gamble, the consumer products giant, has proven to be masterful at rejuvenating core brands and driving their growth. A recent description of the moves that have been made to make laundry detergent Tide a high-growth brand included innovations in product positioning, packaging, the size of the products, usage (to increase cold-water washing, for instance), and branding adjacent products such as the Tide "stain stick." Given that the brand is responsible for $3 billion in sales in the North American market alone, to create a powerful growth engine from it was a remarkable achievement.[3] While many of these types of projects are innovative, by and large the uncertainties within them are moderate, and the projects can be planned using conventional tools.

Platform Launches and Adjacencies

Platform launches are major initiatives, often requiring substantial investment, to establish your firm in a new growth area at scale. The goal of a platform project is, as the name suggests, establishing a platform for significant growth in future revenues and profits. By definition, these projects are inherently more risky than core enhancements, because platforms require that a firm explore new capabilities and new market areas, often at the same time. Platforms are also highly vulnerable. Often, we've seen new platforms struggle in internal power plays with core business projects, which nibble (or sometimes gobble) away at the resources that are supposed to be driving the new platform projects. This phenomenon was what led IBM to create its emerging business opportunity, or EBO, program, as we mentioned in chapter 1. The EBO program makes sure that resources dedicated to platform launches stay that way. Potential platforms can also suffer from premature launch—as when technologies or concepts get bandied about as the next big thing, but no one has actually created a business model for them. Radio-frequency identification (RFID) technology for use in mass logistics and baggage-handling programs comes to mind— though people have talked about these applications since the late

1980s, the right combination of technology capability, market demand, and application design has not yet come together to make this a fast-growth sector.

Successful platforms open up entirely new areas of endeavor for a firm and often create new product or service categories as well. Microsoft's venture into gaming, with its Xbox line of products, might be considered a new platform for the business-oriented software giant. Apple's foray into cellular phones created a new platform beyond computers and music devices. Procter & Gamble's introduction of new, hybrid types of products such as the Swiffer line of cleaning implements creates not only a new brand but the potential for innumerable line extensions. Even agricultural equipment maker John Deere has enjoyed very rapid growth in an entirely new—new for John Deere—type of product: selling GPS-enabled automatic guidance systems to facilitate greater efficiency among its farming customers.

Options for Tomorrow's Growth

Core-enhancement launches and new platform launches represent the here-and-now of investments in growth. In these areas, traditional concepts of planning and management are still worthwhile (although the newer or more uncertain the opportunity, the more you'll want to incorporate discovery-driven principles). Going out yet a little further in terms of uncertainty from today's business are investments in what we call real options. *Real options*, or "seeds," as Amazon.com's Bezos has called them, are investments in businesses, but not investments to achieve a near-term payback. They are, instead, investments in learning.

Specifically, an option is a relatively small investment that creates the right, but not the obligation, to make a further investment later on.[4] Options reasoning provides the financial logic for discovery-driven growth in much the same way that net-present-value calculations provide a financial logic for businesses that are more conventional. The idea is to contain risk by limiting your downside, while maximizing the value you can capture on the upside. Thus, even though you may not be able to calculate precise values, you can distinguish between more and less attractive investment opportunities using real-options reasoning.

Most managers intuitively think in options-oriented ways when they are moving into new areas. Thus, they will beta-test software before officially launching it, do a market test before a full-scale introduction, and create a pilot plant before committing to full-scale production. In two areas, however, executives commonly fail to manage their options effectively. The first is that they impose the same planning, control, and budgeting systems on options that they do on other operations of the corporation. This makes no sense—if you had enough information to run an option that way, it wouldn't be an option.

A second way of mismanaging options is to undercut their benefits by the way you fund projects. The point of a real option is to make small investments before large ones so that the cost of failing is reduced should you find out that the idea isn't going to work. Keep your failures cheap, and you can afford a lot of them. In many companies, however, perverse incentives lead managers to try to obtain all their funding up front, which means that if the projects fail, the failures are large, risks expand, and the motivation to stop and rethink the strategy is eliminated.

So although core-enhancement and platform launches can benefit from traditional planning and management, the more uncertain any project, the more it would benefit from real-options reasoning. The following steps outline how a manager would apply this special type of financial logic.

Apply real-options reasoning as the core discovery-driven investment principles. Instead of following the traditional investment route, discovery-driven principles focus on flexibility and learning:

- Make sure all investments have high upside potential—if you do succeed, the success will be worthwhile.

- Make sure the investment required to determine the potential is relatively small.

- Make sure that you can stop making further investments.

- Invest in a portfolio of ideas.

- Stage and sequence funding so that you review the investment regularly across time.

These recommendations are in contrast to the classic discounted cash-flow view of investment, in which projects are evaluated as though all significant parameters are known, and often funded through to project completion. While it may work for more certain capital projects and core enhancements, discounted cash-flow analysis isn't a good idea for high-uncertainty initiatives. For these initiatives, real-options reasoning is the equivalent of a discounted cash-flow type analysis.

Contain the downside and amplify the upside to pursue opportunities with low risk. Good entrepreneurs are stingy with their money, for a reason. The cheaper your projects are, the less risky they will be and the less you have to lose in the event of a disappointment. Resist the temptation to engage in what we call a *train start*, in which you build up costs before you have a chance to build up revenue streams. Smart companies will instead try to *flow build*, in which costs are incurred only as opportunities to create revenue are discovered. This is the fundamental principle of the options way of investing—to the extent that your downside is small and contained, the risks you are exposed to are also contained. At the same time, if the ideas are potentially rich in opportunity, you have the chance to access a substantial upside. It's this asymmetry between risk and reward that creates option value and that gives discovery-driven growth such power.

Bad luck versus bad management: fail fast, fail cheap, move on. In discovery-driven growth, it's critically important to distinguish between

make stain-resistant khaki pants for Eddie Bauer, automobile bumpers for Toyota, superior golf clubs for Wilson Sporting Goods Co., and anti-microbial wound dressings for Smith & Nephew. The point is that by making such early-stage investments, companies can begin, at minimal cost and risk, to step their way toward the hopefully large market opportunities that today don't even exist.

Will Current Opportunities Achieve Your Growth Goals?

The first way in which a senior team would use the opportunity portfolio is to gain insight into two questions: (1) what's actually going on in our company in terms of strategic initiatives? and (2) will the initiatives as currently funded and conceived address the growth challenge in our strategic framework?

Effective growth companies have learned to ensure that resources that are supposed to be allocated to new opportunities don't get siphoned back into the core business. As we mentioned, IBM has its EBO program, which protects resources for new businesses from the demands of the core business. Nokia uses structural separation to try to put the right emphasis on novel ideas, housing new businesses in a separate division. Samsung has devoted an entire campus space to teams working on new product designs. Whatever the exact practice, the principle is that you want resources for new things to be spent on new things. Period.

You would be surprised (we often are) at how frequently doing a simple mapping of existing ongoing projects elicits an "I had no idea" response from senior executive teams. What often becomes blindingly clear is the disconnect between the strategy as the senior team has conceived it and the actual budget and project approval decisions that determine which initiatives are getting real attention and which are not. Consider, for instance, the portfolio map we discovered in assessing the major development priorities of a global materials company (figure 3-2). This version (which has been stylized to eliminate confidential information) shows each major initiative as a bubble. Its size represents the potential upside that someone has assessed for it. These are all positive-NPV projects (projects with positive net present value). The strategy of the firm is to drive organic growth by commercializing scientific discoveries.

What became obvious as we assessed this portfolio was that the strategy and the actual projects being undertaken were not at all aligned. Scientists in the company felt they were doing their jobs by coming up with miraculous new discoveries, many of which were in the stepping-stone area of the portfolio. Simultaneously, line managers were rewarded for delivering solid numbers within the context of their own strategic business units. There were no strategic levers, processes, or rewards to make sure that someone was managing the next-generation platform investments. No one minded working on the science, since that was considered honorable and failures were tolerated. No one minded working on the core business, since that was measured and

FIGURE 3-2

A portfolio with some important gaps

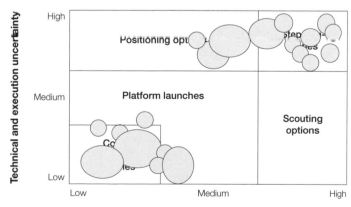

rewarded and considered low-risk. Yet, working on next-generation platforms was considered risky, personally dangerous, and not of much interest to corporate. Further, the scientists were not pursuing projects with substantial commercial upside—no one had really done an upside analysis of the potential results.

Clearly, this situation was not going to get the company where it wanted to go, which was to achieve double-digit, top-line growth. This analysis (and many others) combined to lead the company to reconfigure its organizational structure, its reward system, and its methodologies for vetting and approving projects. Today, separate growth teams are responsible for platform projects. Each team is headed by an extremely senior executive, who is held accountable for making sure the programs are properly resourced and managed with a high degree of visibility. The good news for this company was that it genuinely did have high-quality opportunities based on its science and technology. What was missing was the appropriate management process. Today, it is struggling with restructuring its core business, but the newer businesses emerging from the new platforms are growing rapidly.

An entirely different, and potentially more dangerous, situation existed in the case of a software company whose products were expensive to install and maintain. Its growth portfolio looked like figure 3-3 when we first started to work with the company.

The company had primarily grown through acquisition and for some time had focused on getting basic operations coordinated and meshed. The focus on operational excellence, however, took its toll on the energy needed to invest in interesting new ideas. As a consequence, virtually all the capital and human talent in the organization was being devoted to enhancing the core and building two relatively modest new platforms, which were necessary simply to meet moves already being made by the company's competition.

Analyzing their portfolio led the CEO and his senior team to launch a fairly aggressive nine-month review of their strategy, with a strong emphasis on identifying opportunities. They eventually identified 26

FIGURE 3-3

Where are the growth opportunities? A conservative portfolio

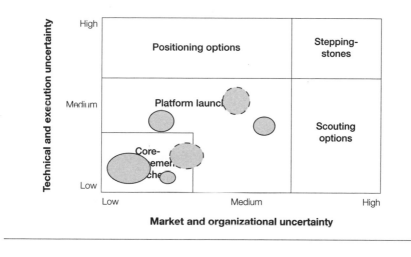

highly attractive opportunity ideas (from over 120 that were discovered). Of these, 7 projects ended up being funded and made the subject of a priority initiative. The senior team members now iterate backward and forward between the frame that they established for meaningful growth (with the end year of 2012 as their aiming point) and progress on the initiatives identified and funded during the strategy work. Managing the total portfolio has also been made a senior team member's main responsibility, and the resources dedicated to it have been set aside from the resources devoted to the core business.

Adopting the Opportunity Portfolio to Drive Growth in the DuPont Bio-Based Materials Business

The opportunity portfolio was deeply important in several major businesses at DuPont. John Ranieri, now vice president and general manager of DuPont Bio-Based materials, adopted the approaches described in this chapter—particularly real-options reasoning and the portfolio approach. In 2002, Ranieri joined the unit of DuPont designated to drive more "green" approaches to its business. Ranieri's corporate-level objective was established by Chad Holliday, who set a target for DuPont to derive 25 percent of its revenue from nondepletable resources by 2010. Ranieri used opportunity mapping to understand and manage dozens of proposed investments that drew on biology, chemistry, materials science, and engineering to develop greener energy sources. Just as we suggest, he made sure that each proposed project was evaluated within its portfolio type and managed using real-options reasoning to contain risk while the team figured out which approaches would be the most fruitful. Five years later, the group had a dozen bio-based materials business opportunities ready for commercialization.

Ranieri offered the following observations on the process:

"The real options framework changes the dynamics of the team and the questions asked," said Ranieri. "For example, here's a question that was not obvious several years ago in the biofuels market: Is there something else we could make that is superior and could be transformative? How can we have both value-added products and reduce the environmental footprint at the same time? It turned out that these qualities weren't mutually exclusive. We opened up new large-market opportunities with the technology base, and as we learned, we found surprises along the way that weren't factored in the original valuations. We won both ways, feeding success and stopping failure simultaneously."

As an example, the answers to those questions resulted in significant new product opportunities—an integrated process that produces cellulosic ethanol from parts of the corn that were formerly waste products and partnered with Broin, and a further partnership with BP to develop biobutanol, which has advantaged performance as a fuel compared to ethanol.

"Being able to ask the right questions at the front-end of innovation is not obvious nor easy," he said. "But when you can more effectively learn and adapt, that's how you get the right answers that create significant value and transform markets."[11]

From Corporate Frame to Project Portfolio: ESCO Revisited

In chapter 2, we showed how ESCO set up its corporate-level strategic growth frame. The company's next step, described on the following pages, was to decide on the portfolio of growth projects that would deliver the desired results.

Initial Opportunity Portfolio for the ESCO Project

The next step in the process was to see whether the initiatives currently under way within ESCO had the potential to generate the desired profit growth. Figure 3-4 shows the results. We found that virtually all the initiatives in place at ESCO were directed toward mostly incremental improvements in the core business. Further, most initiatives were small programs designed to tackle problems facing specific field units. The one large corporate program ESCO was investing in was intended mostly to improve its billing system by advancing its electronic payment and collections capabilities. Important though this was, it was not a growth driver. Like the software company we mentioned earlier, the senior team concluded that it urgently needed to redirect investment toward more promising growth opportunities and to ruthlessly trim some of the less attractive projects.

Over about three months, teams from various ESCO divisions were tasked with developing their very best ideas to drive productivity, increase sales, or, ideally, do both. They were also asked to revisit business

FIGURE 3-4

The opportunity portfolio at ESCO, 2006

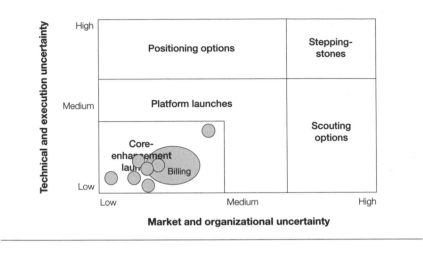

cases for the mostly smaller and incremental projects under way in the field. In preparation for a substantial off-site team meeting, the groups were tasked with preparing rough discovery-driven plans for their best thinking. For the first time, ESCO senior leadership had consistently documented people's ideas on how to improve the business, and the leaders could choose the best of these ideas for implementation. The CEO and senior team then used a two-day off-site meeting with us to crystallize the very best of the ideas and establish the frame for the work that was to follow.

One insight that came out of this off-site meeting was that, given the company's underperformance in ROA and margin terms relative to competitors, significant attention needed to be paid to growing profits through programs aimed at productivity and operational excellence. With operations under control, the leaders could then try to bring up performance in terms of revenue growth. They eventually decided to break down the overall growth challenge into six major initiatives, some oriented toward improvements in productivity and others focused on new sales growth. These initiatives would be plotted on the various areas of the opportunity portfolio, from the aforementioned less uncertain core-enhancement initiatives to the more uncertain positioning and scouting options.

How ESCO's Growth Initiatives Fit on the Opportunity Portfolio

The first key initiative was a program to increase the profitability of the current core business. This initiative would fall in the southwest corner of the opportunity map, as it involves the least amount of uncertainty. The executive in charge was challenged to increase ROA and ROS to target levels in two years, thereby adding $10 million to the profit stream. The objective was to increase profits, not revenues. The senior executive in charge of this initiative divided the challenge into three subprojects: receivables reduction, inventory turn acceleration, and fixed-asset productivity enhancement. Each of these projects in turn was subject to a discovery-driven plan. When going through such an exercise, it's also important to make some decisions about what to stop doing. In the case of ESCO, smaller productivity-enhancing projects that had been under way in ESCO's regional field businesses were stopped to free up resources for the corporate-level activity. While this did lead to some grumbling, the thought process leading to the decision was perceived as transparent, fair, and ultimately quite sensible.

Program 2 was a value-growing platform launch assigned to a senior executive who was charged with building the revenue and particularly profit streams of ESCO's electronic-controls business. This business had been distributing a relatively new family of products that had been growing well and could be poised for rapid and profitable expansion. Again, the executive responsible broke the program into three projects aimed at boosting sales and profits in chemical, refining, and manufacturing sectors, each of which then developed its own discovery-driven plans.

Program 3 was a value-building platform. ESCO had recently added a new family of products from a Japanese vendor. These products were proving to be very popular in the telecom industries, and a senior manager was assigned the task of building revenues at 10 percent compounded while sustaining profit margins. Again, the manager decided to break down the program into several individual projects, each with its own discovery-driven plans.

Both programs 4 and 5 were options programs. Program 4, a positioning option, was to work with a joint project partner to develop a line of intelligent packaging systems products. The systems were aimed at allowing shippers to use RFID to significantly enhance the ability to track and direct shipments of products. For ESCO, the appeal of working on this project was that ESCO itself could benefit from the enhanced logistics. Although the demand for a solution was clear, several alternative systems might have worked out. Since the precise technological solution that would work at the right price point was not understood very well, this initiative was categorized as a set of positioning options (a cluster of small projects aimed at cracking the intelligent packaging area).

Program 5 fell into the scouting-option category. This initiative was precipitated by the recognition that no distribution company of any size could ignore the burgeoning Asian markets, and so there was a strategic imperative to establish initial footholds with a series of trial offers.

Finally, program 6 was assigned to the CFO, who was to begin searching for a high-synergy acquisition that would allow ESCO to "purchase" the profit stream of a smaller firm. The ideal candidate would be a small firm needing an infusion of funds to support its successful growth . . . *but* with the proviso that there be high synergy stemming from this acquisition, which would create an entrée for ESCO into a burgeoning opportunity space. We classified this as an enhancement to the core business, but noted that since it would be to some extent a function of the availability of an attractive acquisition target, it was colored differently than the other, organic growth initiatives.

Figure 3-5 shows what the revised opportunity portfolio looked like at the corporate level for ESCO after the creation of the corporate-level

FIGURE 3-5

The opportunity portfolio at ESCO, 2007

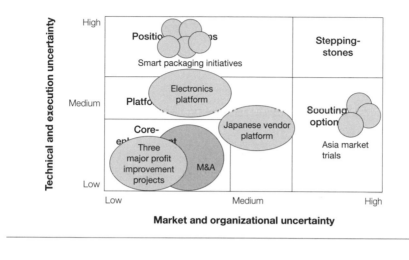

ACTION STEPS

frame. Note that the core initiatives have been consolidated, an acquisition is specifically earmarked for the core, and the portfolio overall has more diversity in terms of the types of new areas the company is pursuing.

In parallel with the mapping work, the senior team laid out its expectations in quantitative terms for the contribution of each initiative to the overall corporate performance. Table 3-1 lays out the suite of projects that they developed. From here on out, the challenge is to design discovery-driven plans to manage and monitor progress for each of these strategic projects.

Let's wrap up this chapter with some specific action steps involving the alignment of your strategy, resource allocation, project approval, and people management practices.

ACTION STEPS

1. Go back to the frame that you developed using the guidelines in chapter 2. You should have from that work an idea of what kind

TABLE 3-1

Growth program portfolio

Initiative	Objective	Impact on 2012 profits	Impact on 2012 revenues
Program 1: Enhance core profits and profitability	Increase core ROA to 10% and ROS to 5.5% in two years	$10,000,000	$ 26,246,748
Program 2: Value-grow electronics	Increase revenues and profits from expansion of electronic control systems	$ 8,000,000	$145,454,545
Program 3: Value-build telecom	Build revenues of telecom switching apparatus	$ 2,000,000	$ 36,363,636
Program 4: Positioning options	Earmark $3 million for intelligent packaging	—	$ 1,000,000
Program 5: Scouting options	Earmark $5 million to to probe Asian market entry	—	$ 2,000,000
Program 6: Acquisitions	Find and acquire high-synergy growth firm	$13,250,000	$220,753,252
	Totals	**$33,250,000**	**$431,818,181**

ROA, return on assets; ROS, return on sales.

of projects of what size and scope would be necessary to address the growth challenges as the senior team currently sees them.

2. Next, collect information on the major initiatives that are currently under way in your firm. You'll have to decide what counts as major, as opposed to business-as-usual. At a minimum, you'll want to know the potential upside of each initiative when it is mature (in terms of either revenue growth, profit growth, efficiency gains, or operational savings). You'll also want to know what resources need to go into the initiative. Then, map the initiatives on to a portfolio map so that you can see

how the whole portfolio looks. As you look at the whole portfolio of initiatives, you'll want to ask yourself some questions:

- Is the portfolio of projects we are actually working on consistent with our strategy?

- Will the current portfolio be adequate to achieve our growth goals?

- Are sufficient resources being dedicated to platform launches and options?

- Are sufficient resources being dedicated to making sure the core is developing well—becoming more efficient and entering into new growth opportunities?

3. Given these insights, decide what proportion of resources you wish to allocate to each area in the opportunity map. There is no one best allocation of resources—it's a function of your strategy. The golden rule, however, is that resources allocated to options stay with options, those allocated to platforms stay with platforms, and so on. You want your very best options to be competing with one another for funding and attention, not options competing with core enhancements.

4. Think through what five to seven initiatives would be necessary to achieve the strategic objectives. Ideally, map these onto the opportunity map so that you can see what proportion of your future effort will come from core enhancements, new platforms, or the conversion of options to platforms. A corporate-level initiative might comprise a number of projects, but at the senior level, you must be clear on the initiatives you intend to support. Some of these might stem from organic growth. Others might involve acquisitions. Since the availability of attractively priced

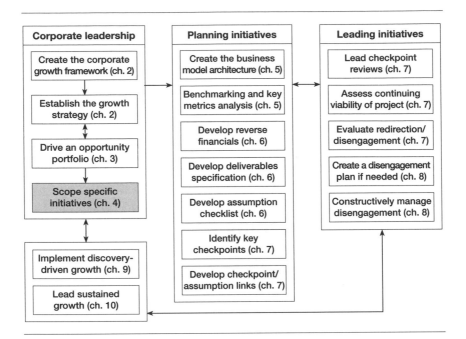

Corporate leadership	Planning initiatives	Leading initiatives
Create the corporate growth framework (ch. 2)	Create the business model architecture (ch. 5)	Lead checkpoint reviews (ch. 7)
Establish the growth strategy (ch. 2)	Benchmarking and key metrics analysis (ch. 5)	Assess continuing viability of project (ch. 7)
Drive an opportunity portfolio (ch. 3)	Develop reverse financials (ch. 6)	Evaluate redirection/ disengagement (ch. 7)
Scope specific initiatives (ch. 4)	Develop deliverables specification (ch. 6)	Create a disengagement plan if needed (ch. 8)
	Develop assumption checklist (ch. 6)	Constructively manage disengagement (ch. 8)
Implement discovery-driven growth (ch. 9)	Identify key checkpoints (ch. 7)	
Lead sustained growth (ch. 10)	Develop checkpoint/ assumption links (ch. 7)	

From Corporate Framing to an Individual Discovery-Driven Plan

By this time, you've seen where the corporate-level framing for discovery-driven growth, or DDG, takes place. In the case of DuPont's KIU system, business leaders defined specific growth arenas within the rubric of the knowledge-intensive growth thrust. For Ingredients, Inc., the strategy was to grow revenues quickly enough to put the company among the top five of competing companies, while maintaining profits at a level sought by the parent corporation. For ESCO, the strategy was to put the company in a position to outperform its competition, improve its productivity, and grow into several highly promising new adjacent areas that showed the promise of expanding the future core business.

Once corporate leadership has defined what success should look like for the whole portfolio of new initiatives it will be pursuing, the next step is to flesh out discovery-driven plans for each of the major initiatives. This involves framing at the level of an individual strategic initiative, at which point a business or project manager might take ownership of the plan, rather than the executive team doing the corporate-level framing. For purposes of simplicity, in the rest of this chapter we will discuss how to do a discovery-driven plan for platform launches and options—since conventional planning is probably going to work just fine for core enhancements and productivity projects (and most companies have well-developed approaches for cost cutting and productivity enhancement).[1] This is the last element of corporate leadership's role in launching DDG, and it is highlighted in our road map on the opposite page.

Getting Started: Establishing the Management Structure for Growth Initiatives

Before developing the plans for individual growth projects, you will want to establish the management structure for your strategic initiatives overall and create the teams that will be doing the actual planning. While there is no one best approach to this task, we have found that firms that are able to maximize the gains they get from their investments in new projects have a few things in common. First, the teams managing strategic growth initiatives are composed of one or more dedicated people whose primary job is driving growth—not part-time people whose primary job is running the core business. Second, there are regular opportunities for the growth teams to connect with leaders in other parts of the organization, often through regular reviews that these leaders attend. Third, there is a mix of knowledge and skill on the teams, with some expertise about the underlying technology or operations of a prospective project combining with other

77

kinds of expertise. Finally, at least a few members of the team should have experience in innovation, venturing, or new-business development.[2] See chapter 9 for additional references on this crucial topic.[3]

With respect to team governance structures, we found that projects work better if they have some degree of independence from the conventional reporting structure of the core business. Some observers refer to this as an *ambidextrous* organization form.[4] Ideally, though, members of the core business would be knowledgeable enough about what is going on in the growth projects that the capabilities created during these projects could be transferred elsewhere in the organization, should that become the best option. It is also vital that resources (budget and people) that are allocated to driving the growth projects don't get siphoned off to the core businesses just because some sort of crisis arises. As we mentioned in chapter 1, IBM discovered that such siphoning was a key reason its projects performed poorly. Once it put mechanisms in place to prevent that from happening (in IBM's case, by appointing a senior-level "godfather" for the projects), it was able to drive growth through its highly successful emerging business opportunity (EBO) program.[5]

Fortis used a similar approach. Though Fortis has been nationalized, we deliberately use it as an example because it shows how even a good growth program can be torpedoed if the firm resorts to ill-advised acquisitions to "buy" growth. What sank Fortis (as well as Wachovia, an otherwise excellently run bank) was a poor acquisition. The problem with growing by acquisition is that the cost of failure is huge, and in the case of both Fortis and Wachovia, one bad acquisition was lethal.

But back to the highly successful Fortis organic growth program. At Fortis, the venturing group reported to the chief strategy officer and was responsible for a whole range of opportunities, from incremental shifts to major acquisitions or partnerships. They had a three-level governance structure that addressed the challenge of giving ventures enough freedom, while linking them to the overall corporation and containing risks. The innovation board consisted of two members of the Fortis executive committee, the chief HR officer, the IT performance manager, and three business unit managers from elsewhere in the company. It approved the funding of the business plans, controlled the robustness of the outcomes, and monitored the strategic fit with the core businesses. The innovation screening committee did rapid evaluations of particular concepts and recommended them to the innovation board. This group consisted of nine high-level managers (or their backups) representing the COO office, operations, insurance, retail banking, commercial banking, finance and control, and overall general management. The innovation network at Fortis facilitated what they called the low-cost "stealing and begging" approach of a corporate venturing department, noting with pride that after seven years of existence, "Fortis Venturing had plus or minus eight hundred ambassadors." In addition, Fortis leveraged an external network of six hundred-plus contact people and appointed individual innovation officers in the core businesses whose job it was to spot and integrate new ideas. Fortis also had a seed fund that could be used to get new ventures started, independent of the normal budgeting process.

Framing the Project

With your team and governance established, you can now turn to the process of actually planning the project. There are five steps involved in creating a frame for a growth project.

1. For each project for which you want to develop a plan, identify what its contribution to profits will have to be *by the time it is generating steady profits* (or steady profit growth). The time frame should reflect the time it will take to get from start-up to steady profit conditions, taking into account the competitive pace of the industry.

2. Determine what the required revenues would have to be if the project is to deliver the specified level of profits and

profitability. You will need to make some assumptions about return on sales and margins. Some firms, by the way, find it more comfortable to begin with revenues and develop an idea about profits from there. Either way can be effective as long as you include numbers in your initial specification.

3. Also specify what the project's profitability should be by this time, recognizing the cold hard fact that you should be getting some risk premium above the current easiest alternative, which is to simply reinvest in the existing business! We generally use return on assets (ROA), because return on investments (ROI) is confounded by your capital structure. However, there is no reason for you not to use ROI or any other measure of profitability that best suits your industry setting.

4. Create a proposed project scope specification that lays out these numbers and their relationship to one another.

5. Calculate a BareBones net present value (NPV) for the project. This NPV will give some indication that it is worth your time to continue with the plan! More on BareBones NPV later.

To illustrate in more depth, instead of continuing with the ESCO (a distribution business) or the toy store (a retail start-up) examples, we'll walk you through the thought process we used to develop a frame for another application: a new business development project within a large industrial manufacturing corporation.

BioBarrier Example: A Growth Initiative for a Large Manufacturing Firm

Our example here is a disguised version of a corporate growth project at a major American corporation. We'll call the initiative the BioBarrier project.

The Corporate Mandate

The BioBarrier project was being considered by a chemical company we'll call MC Chem. At a corporate level, MC Chem was attempting to extend beyond its chemicals roots to build a new position in bioscience products. The company's executive team was particularly keen to get out of commodity chemicals and into more differentiated, higher-margin products. At the corporate level, the senior team specified that a growth platform would look something like this:

> Our platform will develop markets in which we can create a highly differentiated position for either our materials or the delivery vehicle for our materials. The markets should offer at least twice the margin potential of our core business and should be those for which the technical challenges have been overcome. Volume growth matters less than margin growth.

The Invention

MC Chem's researchers had come up with a new product that the advocates within the firm felt might deliver to these requirements. The invention was a new type of disinfecting fluid. The fluid appeared to be about 50 percent more effective than current alternatives in eliminating both bacteria and viruses, with no toxicity to humans and animals. The product could be used on both skin and hard surfaces and could also be dissolved in water. If constituted in a spray-on format, it could be designed to spread evenly on most hard surfaces. At the time we began working with the venturing team, the product had just survived the U.S. Food and Drug Administration (FDA) approval process, meaning that it could validly claim to be a safe disinfectant.

Defining Success

We started building a discovery-driven plan for the BioBarrier project by trying to understand what the project would have to accomplish to make a difference to the corporation's overall performance. Given MC Chem's size (large) and the attractiveness of some of its other investment opportunities, the team felt that a contribution of an additional $10 million in profits was the minimum that would be seen as a win at the corporate level.

MC Chem currently operates in heavily commoditized markets at a ROA figure of about 8 percent. In the industry, this is actually considered a pretty good return and reflects the company's focus on operational excellence. By comparison, the average five-year ROA for the chemical industry is about 4.1 percent, according to Morningstar investment advisers.

The project leaders felt, however, that it would be a mistake to look at this new business with the lens of the existing industry. Instead, they set their sights on pharmaceuticals as a benchmark—an industry with a much more attractive ROI level of 16.5 percent.[6] The leaders sought to do as well as or better than new-product introductions in that industry. What would make an investment in the project truly attractive? They decided to specify a minimum ROA of 33 percent to compensate for the higher risk associated with going into a market new to them with a product that was rather new to them. Similarly taking a cue from the pharmaceutical industry, the team decided to go for a minimum operating margin of 20 percent, recognizing that as incumbents fought back and competitors imitated, this margin might get squeezed.

Initial Frame for BioBarrier project

By doing a few simple calculations, we could now initially specify what would represent success for the BioBarrier project. Note that the key difference between a conventional plan and a discovery-driven plan is that we start with what must occur for the plan to be considered successful, and work backward into the requirements the business would have to meet. In other words, MC Chem shouldn't even bother investing in this project unless it promises, at steady state (about five years out), to generate at least $50 million in revenues with a maximum of $40 million in costs and no more than $40 million in total assets (table 4-1).

So far, so good—we have a picture of what the business would have to accomplish to be taken seriously as a contributor to MC Chem's growth portfolio. But we still don't know if it will be worthwhile to undertake the journey to the steady-state revenues. To tackle this question, we use a tool we call a BareBones net present value (NPV) calculator.

The Barebones NPV Concept

The BareBones NPV tool is a handy little Excel-based calculator that will provide you with a number analogous to an NPV calculation. NPV is perhaps the most widely used technique to judge whether investment in a new project is warranted. While we (and others) have our problems with it, some managers still find it comforting to have a positive NPV for a proposed project. The number can also help illuminate some of the financial assumptions you are making.

TABLE 4-1

Initial frame for BioBarrier project

Hypothetical specification		Where the number came from
Required profit	$10 million	Specified by management
Required margin	20%	Specified by management
Required revenues at required margin of 20%	$50 million	Calculated from required revenue and required profit
Allowable costs (80% of sales)	$40 million	Calculated by subtracting required profit from required revenue
Required ROA	33%	Specified by management
Allowable assets	$40 million	Calculated by dividing required profits by required ROA

ROA, return on assets.

83

Key Variables

Calculating an NPV can be a time-consuming and fiddly exercise. For the purposes of discovery-driven planning, however, you can achieve roughly right results with a pared-down version of NPV. The beauty of BareBones NPV is that instead of laboriously calculating year-by-year spreadsheets over the entire life of the project, you need to estimate only nine project values:

1. *Launch time:* How long will it be before the project begins to generate its first revenues?

2. *Ramp-up time:* How long will it take the project to move from its first revenues to a steady state? The BareBones NPV estimator will assume that this is a linear ramp-up period.

3. *Competitive response time:* How long after launch will it take for competitors to respond?

4. *Competitive erosion time:* How long will it take for the competitors to erode your profits to the point that you are only just recovering your fixed costs? The BareBones NPV estimator will assume that profits drop off linearly from the start of the competitive response time to the end of the erosion time.

5. *Total investment:* What is the expected total investment? The BareBones NPV estimator will assume that this is a onetime investment incurred at the end of the launch time.

6. *Discount rate:* This number is used to "discount" future cash flows to account for the fact that if you weren't doing this project, you could just as easily leave your money in a bank account and earn interest. The idea is that a sum of money in your pocket today is worth more than the same amount five years from now,

because today's money could earn interest. If you don't know the rate for your firm, your finance people should be able to give you this (and they might insist that you adjust it upward for risk, as well). They might refer to it as the *cost of capital*, but the idea is the same—using money for your project means you can't use it for something else, and unless your project offers better returns than a savings account does, the cost of capital is a value-destroyer for your firm.

7. The expected annual fixed costs at steady state.

8. The expected annual variable cost per unit at steady state.

9. The expected annual revenues in units at steady state.

You can download the calculator tool from the Web site for this book, at www.discoverydrivengrowth.com, as well as from Rita's Web site: www.ritamcgrath.com.

The BareBones analysis gives you a simple, rough-but-ready estimate of the NPV of the project for comparison with competing projects. Unless the investment, ramp-up, and erosion profiles are bizarre, nothing more accurate than a BareBones NPV is really needed for uncertain investments. Why? Since we already know that the estimate is roughly wrong, why bother spending energy and effort refining it? After all, what is the point of being precisely wrong—to four decimal places? Further, if someone suggests that the project may take longer to get to steady state, or that competition may enter sooner, or the fixed costs may be higher, or any other of the nit-picky questions you may get at a presentation, you have an easy response. You can challenge nit-pickers to say what their number is, enter it into the BareBones estimator, and—bang!—in seconds, you have the revised NPV.

Let's illustrate how we developed the BareBones NPV calculation for the BioBarrier project.

BioBarrier: An Example of BareBones NPV

Here's how we came up with the BareBones numbers for the BioBarrier project:

- We used the specifications in table 4-1 to frame the cost and asset numbers at their highest value (to be on the conservative side). We also used the numbers from the table to project revenues. (This doesn't mean that the revenues will be this number, just that if they are, the project withstands the test of time value of money.)

- The initial investment is $30 million.

- Assuming that, like the existing business, fixed costs are 10 percent of total cost and variable costs are therefore 90 percent of total allowable costs, this gives fixed costs of $4 million and variable costs of $36 million.

- Time to launch, including plant construction, is two years, based on previous experience.

- Time to ramp up from launch to steady state is two years.

- Time to competitive entry after launch is seven years (the FDA approval time is about six years, during which time competitors will not be able to offer a copycat product).

- Time from competitive entry to competitive erosion of profits is eight years.

- So, the lifespan after launch is fifteen years (eight plus seven).

- Assume the current discount rate is 15 percent.

Figure 4-1 shows you how this input would look when entered into the spreadsheet tool. It gives you an illuminating summary of the whole project in one snapshot and allows you to do what-ifs in seconds.

FIGURE 4-1

BareBones specification for BioBarrier project (million dollars)

Stage 1: Product launch	
Initial investment at launch:	$30
Years from today to project launch:	2
Annual fixed costs:	$4
Annual fixed revenues:	$0
Stage 2: Product reaches steady state	
Years from launch to steady state:	2
Annual variable costs in steady state:	$36
Annual variable revenues in steady state:	$50
Stage 3: Entrance of competitors	
Years from launch to competitive entrance:	7
Years from competitive entrance to competitive erosion:	8
Stage 4: Product termination	
Project lifespan (from launch to termination):	15
Project rate of return:	15%

You can see how the numbers are expected to unfold over time in figure 4-2. The BareBones will use these numbers and calculate a positive NPV of $7.69 million for BioBarrier, which suggests that the project is worth considerable further work.

A Negative BareBones NPV: Perhaps All You Need to Kill an Idea Early

If your BareBones NPV comes out negative, you have not failed. It just means that you could drop the project and deploy your people's creative talent to another, more promising project.

One of the real benefits of starting off planning a specific initiative with a clear frame is that sometimes, before you invest any money or time at all, it's obvious that an idea just isn't going to work or that you need a lot more information before you can confidently proceed. We

FIGURE 4-2

Steady-state expectation profile

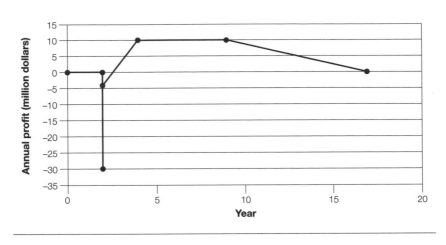

do this all the time in our entrepreneurship classes—we force our students to be realistic about whether a particular business even has the potential to drive exceptional growth and returns.

One example is a case of a proposed entrepreneurial venture to sell sliding-door openers as a retrofit for existing homes. The original concept was to sell kits to install the door openers for people who would want them so a person could, for instance, carry food or drinks from the kitchen to the outdoor patio without having to wrestle with an unwieldy sliding door. When we ran through the framing part of the plan, it pretty quickly became clear that a product like this wouldn't be of much interest to the major distribution channels (such as Lowe's or The Home Depot), because volumes would probably be too small. To sell such kits through specialty retailers, such as Hammacher Schlemmer, might not have generated enough volume to create manufacturing efficiencies. Finally, in doing some background research, we learned that such products do actually exist—they are designed to be used by persons with disabilities and are priced in the hundreds, or even thousands, of dollars and require modifications to the door, the door frames, and, sometimes, the supporting structures of the home. At that point, our potential entrepreneur decided there would be easier ways to earn a living and moved on to another project. At the time that decision was made, the total investment was about three hours of time, a little Internet research, and some phone calls. How much better than spending time, emotion, and credibility doing "market research," or—God forbid—raising money, only to find out the hard reality later on.

Moving On from Framing

Each project that is part of your major growth thrust should be framed like the way the BioBarrier case was framed, so that everyone is completely clear on what success would look like at project maturity and what the key financial assumptions are. It's important to remember that these are still only assumptions, because you will almost certainly find yourself revising them as you go along.

The next step in the process is to take each strategic project and give some serious thought to the unit of business and key metrics that will comprise the business architecture for each one.

ACTION STEPS

1. Determine where you are going to locate your projects and what governance structure you plan to use for them.

2. Pull together the team that will constitute the planning body for your project. We discuss this further in chapter 9. Charge specific managers with the responsibility for the execution of each project plan. Make clear who must monitor, redirect, and report on the progress of their individual plan as it unfolds. Our recommendation is that major platforms require a dedicated

resource—more modest core enhancement and some options projects can be done on a part-time basis.

3. For all the projects, each team should obtain the specification of success developed for them at a corporate level. From the last chapter, your strategy should clearly specify the initiatives—both for growth and for productivity enhancement—that are desirable. You should have separate initiatives to grow platforms, enhance core businesses, and create options for future growth.

4. Work through the five steps of putting together a hypothetical frame. What you want is a clear understanding of required profits, ROI, and allowable costs.

5. For each project, do a BareBones NPV calculation. If it isn't positive, consider replacing the original project with one that might have higher potential, or spend some time imagining what it would take to enhance the BareBones NPV. If enough of the projects don't look as though they will sum up to the corporate growth challenge, you may need to loop back with the executive team to revisit the corporate-level frame.

II

Executing
Specific Growth
Opportunities

In this part of the book, we focus on how to drive specific individual growth initiatives by using discovery-driven-planning principles. The sum total of all the initiatives needs to deliver to the overall strategic frame that was established in the first part of the book. Part 2 provides specific guidance to work through the issues for a given project and recalls that early, cheap failures are not a bad thing, nor is project redirection. Note that you would follow the procedures in the next three chapters for every major growth initiative that is outside the core business, but is part of your strategic growth framework.

CHAPTER FIVE

Designing the Business Model Architecture

We ended the last part of the book by framing the results a particular initiative would have to deliver in order to be considered successful in the corporate portfolio. In this chapter, we show you how a specific project can be evaluated within this overall strategic framework. We'll cover four key ideas: (1) establishing the viability of a business, given corporate requirements; (2) analyzing the unit of business; (3) analyzing the nearest competitive offer; and (4) identifying subsequent key metrics. The idea is that very early on, you need to get extremely practical and real about the proposed business as a business (and not just as a cool idea).

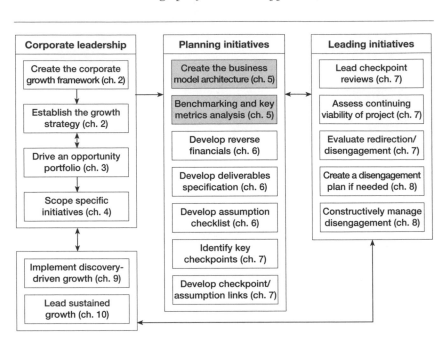

Corporate leadership	Planning initiatives	Leading initiatives
Create the corporate growth framework (ch. 2)	Create the business model architecture (ch. 5)	Lead checkpoint reviews (ch. 7)
Establish the growth strategy (ch. 2)	Benchmarking and key metrics analysis (ch. 5)	Assess continuing viability of project (ch. 7)
Drive an opportunity portfolio (ch. 3)	Develop reverse financials (ch. 6)	Evaluate redirection/ disengagement (ch. 7)
Scope specific initiatives (ch. 4)	Develop deliverables specification (ch. 6)	Create a disengagement plan if needed (ch. 8)
	Develop assumption checklist (ch. 6)	Constructively manage disengagement (ch. 8)
Implement discovery-driven growth (ch. 9)	Identify key checkpoints (ch. 7)	
Lead sustained growth (ch. 10)	Develop checkpoint/ assumption links (ch. 7)	

You need to develop such an architecture for every major growth project that you're depending on to deliver your corporate growth program. For each growth initiative, you should now have a project frame. Now we will look at what is needed to turn the frame into a reality.

Discovery-driven framing is invaluable for figuring out the scope of a proposed growth initiative and defining whether the effort will be worthwhile. For this reason, it is a very popular tool with venture capitalists and is frequently taught in university-based entrepreneurship courses. As you can see from the road map above, this chapter begins the transition from a focus at the strategy level to a focus on individual initiatives.

Before showing you how to move from the framing exercise illustrated in the BioBarrier project, we need to spend a little time on how you would create the basic business model. We like to start by defining the unit of business.

The Foundation of Business Architecture: The Unit of Business

The fundamental architecture of a discovery-driven plan is established with the selection of a unit of business that will drive the revenue and profits of the business. The *unit of business* refers quite simply to what you decide the customer is going to be paying you for. This foundational decision shapes just about everything else that influences the way the business will unfold. The unit of business for which your customer is willing to pay has major implications for how you price, where profits come from, what your earnings logic is, and how you configure your operations.

For most manufactured products, defining the unit is straightforward because it's a physical unit of something you sell, as we saw with the toy store example in chapter 1. In that example, the toy store could make many more opportunities to generate revenues than just by selling individual toys. For instance, the company could extend the offer by designing new experiences (such as toy fairs, conventions, or trunk shows). A toy party like the old Tupperware parties might extend the brand beyond the limits of a physical store.

Many businesses can benefit from exploring alternative business units, or more nuanced ones. Consider your cell phone: while the phone manufacturer's business plan revolves around unit sales of phones, for the operator that sells you the phone and the service that makes it connect, the unit is subscription revenue or number of calls placed, or both. Depending on which company you are, it might be more or less attractive to give away something another company might charge for, in order to sell more units in your model. Apple, for instance, gives away the iTunes Music Store software for free because the giveaway facilitates the sale of iPod music players, which are highly profitable for the company.

Finding New Opportunities by Redefining the Unit of Business

Sometimes, radically new opportunities open up when you can think of ways to change the unit of business, particularly if you can link the way customers pay you to an outcome that is desirable or salient to them. To stick with the cell phone example, huge new growth was prompted when the concept of a prepaid phone card jumped from conventional telephony to mobile telephony—a jump that some suggest occurred in 2001.[1]

The advantage of prepaid was that for certain customer segments, an open per-usage account or even a monthly subscription was too scary, too expensive, or too inconvenient. These selfsame consumers, however, were more than glad to pay far higher prices per minute for a pay-as-you-go approach to cell usage. Offering so-called prepaid phone cards allows users to limit their spending; avoid service contracts and, sometimes, expensive extras; and in general increase their flexibility. The prepaid concept has now spawned a whole group of secondary industries in which participants offer machines that will "top off" your cell phone minutes while you are on the go.

Many innovations today are essentially business model, or unit-of-business, innovations. When Apple Computer, with its free iTunes music software, facilitated purchasing music by the song, rather than by the album, it created great strain among traditional production firms (and allowed Apple to avoid agonizing about digital music piracy). At the same time, the by-the-song model opened up enormous new opportunities for independent and less mainstream music labels as well as yielded gold from the established companies' backlists by making single-song purchases available to those wanting only that old song and not an album of unwanted extra songs. For another, more detailed example of business-model innovation, see the box "Shaking Up the Flower Business with a Different Business Model" on page 100.

Some units of business are inherently more or less attractive than others. For instance, a onetime sale of a total solution means less recurring revenue than the repeated sales of sets of transactions. Table 5-1 summarizes recent examples of companies that are driving their growth through different business models than they had been pursuing previously.

Let's take a concrete example to see how unit-of-business innovation can change an industry. In this case, it's the video rental business. In the late 1990s, companies in the video rental industry used a nearly identical business model. People rented movies on VHS tapes for a certain amount per day and were assessed a fee if they returned the movie late. Although late fees were profitable for video rental chains (by some estimates, garnering up to 20 percent of their total revenue stream), the fees often enraged customers.[2] Reed Hastings, the subsequent founder of Netflix, ran afoul of this situation:

> I had a big late fee for *Apollo 13*. It was six weeks late, and I owed the video store $40. I had misplaced the cassette. It was all my fault. I didn't want to tell my wife about it. And I said to myself, "I'm going to compromise the integrity of my marriage over a late fee" . . . I started thinking, "How come movie rentals don't work like a health club, where, whether you use it a lot or a little, you get the same charge?"[3]

Interestingly, the original Netflix business model wasn't so different from the video-store model. At its launch in 1998, Netflix changed only the distribution method; instead of having customers go to a physical location to pick out and rent a movie, Netflix delivered a DVD to them through the mail for a five-dollar fee. Customers still incurred late fees if they returned the DVD late. Results were disappointing and precipitated a redirection. Out of desperation, the young company went with the "health club" model. As Hastings recalled, "What gave us the courage to switch was the necessity to switch."[4]

At the time, prevailing wisdom held that customers preferred the video-store model because watching a movie was an impulse buy. Reed and his team rethought this assumption. What if the impulsive

---

Shaking Up the Flower Business with a Different Business Model

Proflowers is the brainchild of Jared Polis, who founded the wildly popular, free greeting-card Web site www.bluemountain.com. In 1998, he explored the idea of offering flowers for sale on the site, leveraging the presence he had established with the 54 million unique visitors who regularly sent free e-cards from his site. Polis, however, conceived of an entirely different way of selling flowers than the traditional approach. In the conventional business, flowers are shipped from growers, stored in a warehouse, distributed to florists, and then delivered by van or car when a central agency, such as Teleflora, forwards an order to the florist.

Polis reasoned that the Internet could be leveraged to take advantage of entirely different key metrics. In his system, orders are received either over the Internet or by phone and dispatched to growers who are part of the network. The growers fill orders directly, using packaging provided by Proflowers. Shipping is handled by carriers such as Federal Express and UPS, and the flowers are shipped directly to their destination.

Of course, nothing stays the same, and Netflix continues to evolve its model. A new feature supports a video on-demand format to compete with alternative distribution vehicles (such as shows that can be downloaded to iPod players). Indeed, Comcast has just announced a major commitment to supporting a huge library of video on-demand programming, much of it in high definition, a potentially powerful competitor to Netflix's own video-streaming offer. Clearly, it will soon be time to revisit the unit-of-business question in the video rental business once more.

This is why we suggest that you include expected competitive response and profit erosion time in the BareBones NPV calculation. To grow in today's markets, you must keep innovating and thinking of your follow-up innovations even as you launch your current ones. You

The Proflowers model changes the following key metrics entirely:

- Costs to create customer awareness (marketing)
- Distribution costs
- Inventory costs
- Packaging costs
- Inventory age and losses due to spoilage
- Speed to delivery
- Gross margins

The business model disintermediates brokers, wholesalers, and retail florists, allowing the company to offer consumers a price break while maintaining high margins. One analyst reported that the company enjoyed twice the profit margins of conventional florists, over 15 percent, compared with around 7 percent. A recent analyst report estimated that Proflowers has a 20 percent share of the online and telephone floral gift market, up from under 15 percent in 2002.[a]

[a] C. Bibb, "PRVD: Disruptive Business Model That Is Taking Share; 52% Upside Potential; Initiating Coverage with a Buy Rating," June 20, 2005, WR Hambrecht + Co., www .wrhambrecht.com.

simply cannot do this using the conventional tools. If you are going to continue launching uncertain new initiatives to keep up with the changes imposed by market forces, you have to be able to spell out a future, plan it flexibly, and either follow the evolving success path or fold at low cost. Therefore, discovery-driven growth.

So, as you can see, selecting the unit of business can have formidable consequences. Therefore, don't fix on a unit too early! Think about alternative units, especially those that make it easier and less risky for the customer to switch from the current pattern of purchasing to buying from you. Or think about units in which the competitors are embedded in systems that are difficult or uncomfortable to change in response to your business model. Or ideally, think about both!

Four Specific Steps to Identify Alternative Units of Business

So, how do you begin to identify alternative units of business for your new opportunities? Here are four steps we have found that work well:

1. Consider which primary needs your offering addresses and which customer segments find those needs important.

2. Analyze how well the existing solutions are meeting those needs. What are the drawbacks with the existing solutions, from the customers' point of view?

3. Consider whether these alternatives also benefit from some shift in the external environment that could give you an advantage over existing solutions (in the case of Netflix, the shift to the DVD format as opposed to videocassettes made the postage-based model feasible). If you can see a way of taking advantage of new developments while your competitors are still committed to legacy operations, it can open up a new opportunity space for you.

4. Brainstorm alternative ways of meeting customers' needs— alternatives that don't suffer from the same drawbacks that hurt the existing model. It's particularly powerful if you can conceive of a way of serving customers who today aren't served, because of expense or another barrier to adoption.

This process usually leads to a number of possible alternative units of business. For a complex business, it's usually worthwhile to redo the framing exercise, considering your alternative options as you go.

From Construction Materials to Problems as Customers Experience Them

Executives at DuPont used the Knowledge-Intensive University (KIU) approach to drive DuPont's extremely successful venture into what they initially called "weatherization," but which later became their "building innovations." The venture was a true exploration of alternative units of business for DuPont. As part of the company's thrust toward more knowledge-intensive growth and away from pure materials, in early 2002 the group went through the KIU process that we described in chapter 2.

As the project team learned more about builders' concerns, it became clear that concerns such as moisture prevention, water management, damage control from wind and severe weather, and protecting inhabitants in the event of tornadoes and hurricanes were all issues that no one provider addressed, but that lent themselves to solutions featuring DuPont technology. Tom Schuler, the product manager at the time and now vice president and general manager of building innovations, described how the shift in emphasis led to a change in the fundamental unit of business at the company:

> If you look at where we were when we started talking to customers, the business was about water management. That's what customers told us they valued: "Help us to manage the water in a building system and deal with problems of mold and mold remediation." We found out that just being able to supply rolls of Tyvek was insufficient. We had to put together a complete water management system instead of providing just one element of it. So the market for us has changed from us competing against other roll goods companies to us competing against other water management systems, where the core capability is understanding how the whole building works. The good news is we've added this capability and still have an edge in the building science.[7]

DuPont eventually developed FlexWrap to prevent rain damage around window and door openings, DuPont StormRoom to protect families during tornados, and SentryGlas to safeguard homes from hurricane damage.[8] The change in unit of business created a significant growth engine for DuPont, as the way the products went to market was much better aligned with customers' needs and concerns.

Since 2001, the unit has enjoyed an annual compound growth rate of over 20 percent, even in times when the building and construction materials markets were flat or down.

In reflecting on this experience years later, Schuler observed that the unit-of-business insight was key to the success of his business and has changed the way he thinks about future proposals:

> One of the first things I do now is do that commonsense test. If I look at a unit of business and my plan over five years, I ask if it is realistic to assume that I can build an offering with building blocks that I have clearly defined. Is it realistic to assume that growth can occur based on that model? The most valuable aspect to me is the quantification of growth, of being required to tie it directly to a product or an activity. The biggest things we got out of the process are [twofold]: quantifying the drivers in the strategy to a quantifiable unit of business, and secondly, making sure that it would be sustainable. Just doing something once is not enough to have a sustainable business.[9]

Schuler also observed that it was critically important for the business to be able to go forward with a consistent strategy, just as we argued in chapter 3: "If you fundamentally look at the strategy we laid out back in 2002, it didn't change. To me, that's a hallmark of a reasonable strategy and, hopefully, good business practice. If your strategy is changing year to year, you don't have a strategy."[10]

Evaluating a Complex Business: Back to the BioBarrier Case

Let's recall the frame for BioBarrier that we introduced in chapter 4. The most important number to bear in mind at the moment is the $50 million in required revenue that the business has to be able to generate when it is mature (table 5-3).

As we suggested to them, the members of the BioBarrier team deliberately took the time to first consider alternative units of business.

TABLE 5-3

Recap: Initial frame for BioBarrier project

Specifications of the business		Where the number came from
Required profit	$10 million	Specified by management
Required margin	20%	Specified by management
Required revenues at required margin of 20%	$50 million	Calculated from required revenue and required profit
Allowable costs (80% of sales)	$40 million	Calculated by subtracting required profit from required revenue
Required ROA	25%	Specified by management
Allowable assets	$40 million	Calculated by dividing required profits by required ROA

ROA, return on assets.

Among the alternatives they evaluated were selling disinfecting services on an outsourced basis to hospitals, providing training services, and selling the disinfecting chemicals to packaged-goods companies that made cleaning supplies.

In the services model, the business would contract with a hospital to provide disinfection of specific areas, such as the operating rooms. After considering it carefully, the team concluded that this model was unattractive for two reasons. First, it would vastly increase the logistical complexity of MC Chem's operations—indeed, the fluid would be one of the least of the company's costs if MC Chem decided to go into the outsourced disinfection business. Second, when the project team looked at how disinfectants were used, it found that in general, they were used by the people hired to do the cleaning. MC Chem had no interest in going into the business of outsourcing general hospital-cleaning services, an even lower-margin business than their core and one in which they had no particular expertise. Finally, replacing the cleaning services currently used by hospitals would involve displacing entrenched vendors in a business that was unknown to MC Chem. So it rejected that model. It also considered selling disinfecting solutions to cleaning services, but concluded that the cleaning services firms didn't have the technical capability to judge how effective the solution was. MC Chem also briefly considered offering the active ingredient in BioBarrier to other companies for inclusion in their products, but rejected this idea because it didn't fit the corporate strategy of moving into a more powerful position in the value chain, rather than being an ingredient supplier.

Note that the plan for any strategic project should always be assessed in light of the corporate frame and the corporate strategy, lest it be rejected at that level. In this case, MC Chem thus decided to go with a unit of business that was familiar both to the company and to its prospective customers: namely, disinfecting fluid sold by the gallon.

Selecting a Tentative Target Customer Segment

Having picked a tentative unit of business, the team could then turn to assessing the opportunity. Are the ambitious goals feasible? Before we can answer that question, we need to make some choices about which customer group to target. In BioBarrier's case, the planning team considered sales to at least three major markets. The first represents those end users and consumers who would buy the disinfectant fluid for home or office use. They typically buy through retail channels. The second market is the industrial segment. These firms, such as food processors, restaurant chains, and manufacturers of sensitive materials (such as medical devices), buy their disinfectant fluid through industrial supply channels. The third segment consists of hospitals, which typically buy through hospital suppliers.

It is critically important to know who actually dominates the purchasing decision as you work through this part of the process. For BioBarrier, individual consumers decide for themselves, while for industrial buyers and hospitals, the predominant decision maker would be a purchasing manager responsible for supplies.

Since the product is new and from a newcomer to the disinfectant market, BioBarrier will have to overcome the challenges of complete lack of awareness and skepticism on the part of consumers and industrial distributors. Gaining that awareness can be expensive, particularly for a business whose parent company expects the ultimate business to be a large one. Furthermore, until the genuine superiority of BioBarrier is established, it's easier for customers to simply continue to do what they have always done, rather than switch to something unknown. We find, by the way, that entrepreneurs are almost always excessively optimistic about the enthusiasm that prospective customers are going to display on the basis of a product's technical merits.

Hospital buyers, on the other hand, are all too well aware of the risks of a disinfectant failure in their facilities. Should they have such a failure, it's potentially a business (and a human) disaster. Such buyers are therefore a lot more likely to consider a more effective treatment, provided that they can be brought to believe the argument made by the provider.

An assumption made by the BioBarrier team was, therefore, that hospitals and their associated medical schools make their purchasing decisions on the basis of technical specifications and have the capacity to test just how good the solution is. A further assumption is that such buyers will look beyond standard pricing to determine the efficacy of the application for the price charged. In other words, if the solution is more expensive, but more efficacious (ideally producing savings elsewhere in the system), these customers will be open to purchasing the product. Meet the higher quality at a competitive price, and you have a chance of breaking into the order process.

Current competitors sold disinfectants by the gallon at a price of about $55 per gallon. This creates an opportunity: if BioBarrier is genuinely more effective, perhaps the team could slightly undercut existing solutions, selling at a list price of $50 per gallon (we will return to this pricing issue later).

Given the requirement for $50 million in revenues, at $50 per gallon, the company would need to sell one million gallons. That's a pretty big business. These numbers first suggest that this business has to be prepared to be national, if not global, in its operations. In fact, if you assume a 250-day working year, the implication is that this business at maturity has to be able to sell four thousand gallons per day. Is that an unrealistic number? Well, let's apply the same kind of analysis here that we did with the toy store and consider the project feasibility in terms of customer demand.

According to published sources, there are 5,794 hospitals in the United States.[11] If we assume that when the BioBarrier business is mature, MC Chem can aspire to serving 25 percent of these hospitals with its disinfecting products (a very aggressive goal), that means its target market is some 1,449 hospitals. Each of these will have to purchase, on average, 690 gallons of BioBarrier disinfectant annually, or about 57 gallons a month. According to the University of California–Irvine Medical Center inventory manager, who was kind enough to respond to our phone call, the hospital uses 40 to 50 gallons of disinfectant per month for antibacterial surface treatment. Oops.

If one of the largest potential customers for the product would not, on average, use enough of an existing offer to meet our profit objectives, that means we're going to need to serve more hospitals than the 25 percent of the American market we assumed the business could capture. The team assumed that 25 percent was the maximum market share it could realistically aspire to hold. This suggests the plan for the business would have to go beyond the domestic market, targeting hospitals in other parts of the world. This has massive implications for the scope of the business—but at least we've figured this out before too much investment was made.

Should we consider dropping BioBarrier at this stage? Not necessarily. First, we need to look at competition: to think through the market implications of BioBarrier, we need to consider competing alternatives. This brings us to some hard thinking about the true competition to the BioBarrier offer and the next piece of analysis you might want to do.

Competitive Benchmarking: Can You Win?

Connecting the strategic frame to the business frame helps you think through two key issues. The first is whether your proposed new business has the potential to deliver to the desired outcome as you have framed it. If it doesn't show the potential to do that at this early stage, for goodness' sake, move on to something else. The second issue is whether your assumptions about customer adoption are realistic. To think this through, you need to look at how well your business as designed stacks up against the competition, from the customers' point of view. We call this type of competitive benchmarking the *nearest competitive offer* (NCO) analysis, which forces you to identify how you are going to truly differentiate your offer. It helps to remember that from the customers' point of view, there is always some alternative to what you would like to sell (even if it is living without your solution).

Try to avoid the "there is no competition" pitfall. There is usually some alternative way in which customers are meeting their needs or some alternative option they'd prefer to put their resources into. After all, the money they spend buying from you is money they can't spend on something else, so at a very basic level, there is always going to be competition, even if only for specific resources.

Nearest Competitive Offer (NCO) Analysis

History suggests that true breakthrough products have to meet at least three tests:

- They differentiate massively on some dimension of performance that enough customers really care about (even if they are worse on others).

- They radically change the cost-benefit ratio for customers.

- They change the criteria that customers use to judge value.[12]

There is almost always an existing alternative to breakthrough products that can provide comparative information for the planning process. Take fax machines. The print quality of the early thermal fax machines was, frankly, dreadful. So how did they become so ubiquitous? Because many customer segments didn't care about the quality of the output—they cared about the speed at which an image of a written document could be transmitted. Prior to the introduction of fax technology, the alternatives were conventional mail, overnight delivery services such as Federal Express, very expensive courier services, or telex transmissions.

Consider the attributes of alternatives that might have been germane to the project team working on the fax machine (table 5-4). The NCO analysis suggests that the market for fax machines will depend on the products' ability to deliver relatively inexpensive images of documents faster than mail, more cheaply than overnight delivery, and with less need for user intervention than telex service. Further, the analysis would have pointed out how important market penetration would be. Without a network of fax owners, there was no point in owning one, because there was no one to send a fax to. The academics call this characteristic *network externalities*, and it can make or break a fledgling product category.[13] Indeed, although some of the technologies underlying fax transmission have been around since the 1850s, fax machines did not become popular until after 1983, when a common standard was established for the rate at which faxes would be transmitted.

Table 5-4 makes it clear that the fax machine had the potential to redefine what people would pay for paper-based information transmission. Instead of rich, high-quality output delivered quickly, faxes offered low-quality output delivered instantly, which for many users is good enough for their immediate needs. In fact, by using fax machines, customers could work far more easily with partners in far-flung locations, particularly those without overnight delivery services

110

TABLE 5-4

Comparison of fax and alternatives

Attribute	Mail service	Federal Express	Fax machine	Telex
Speed	Slow (days or weeks)	Overnight	Instantaneous	Instantaneous
Cost of service	Inexpensive	Expensive at $20 per document	Relatively inexpensive— phone time and consumables	Relatively inexpensive
Equipment cost	None	None	Over $2,000 at inception	Significant to acquire equipment and network
Value of having other users	None	None	Huge; requires recipient to have a machine	Huge; requires recipient to have a machine
Amount of information that can be transmitted	Unlimited	Unlimited	Unlimited	Limited by necessity of typing text to recipient
Amount of effort required to send message	High; often means going to the post office and waiting	Minimal; they will pick up from you	Minimal; can be done right in one's own office at any time, machine can be unattended	Medium; requires a correspondent on the other end
Availability	Limited by postal service hours	Limited by overnight cutoffs	Unlimited	Limited by office hours and recipient's being in attendance
Quality	High	High	Low	Low

or reliable local postal service. In this way, fax services were an early contributor to the world-flattening processes of global supply and communication chains. The machines coincidentally took off in sales during the decade in which Japan became a truly important global player, which also increased the demand for efficient communications over long distances.

The point of understanding the NCO is that it can clarify what attributes you assume will attract customers and what kinds of trade-offs these same customers will make. In the case of faxes, having an instant, exact image of a document—be it a draft contract, handwritten note, or résumé—was critically important. NCO analysis will also point out places where your proposed offer is at a disadvantage relative to alternatives. In the case of the fax machine, the cost of acquiring the equipment was a deterrent, as was the need to have a network of users to fax to before the machine had any value. This suggests why early fax adopters were rather large corporations, who could create a value-adding network of branch locations on their own. These customers pulled through demand by requiring suppliers and customers to also work with fax machines.

Modeling Competing Offers Through Consumption-Chain Analysis

Let's see how the concept of competitive benchmarking might play out in the case of the BioBarrier team. As we mentioned, the point of this analysis is to try to understand how your proposed operations will influence the customers' experience. The tool we like to use to work through this is called a *consumption chain*, which we've written about extensively in other books, so we won't belabor the idea here.[14] The key point is that if you want to understand your impact on the customers' experiences, you need to think through their total interaction with your solution, from awareness to selection, payment, financing, usage, service, and eventually disposal of the product or discontinuation of the relationship. We call these experiences *links*.

Often, problems in a new business emerge because some major gap in customer experience nullifies the usefulness of the whole business. For example, in the Iridium project, the Motorola-led consortium for satellite-based phones, the focus was mainly on how the phones would work when used. What was somehow overlooked was how the phones would be sold—the consortium assumed that partners would follow up on leads and distribute the phones internationally, but the necessary capabilities to do this were never put in place. The project is now a poster child for the worst way to develop an innovative venture.

Consumption-chain analysis is a good technique to remind you that just because you are very interested in what you are doing, for the most part, customers aren't. They are interested in getting their own needs met and their own jobs done. Understanding consumption chains is also a good way to get a grasp of how you might add value besides the simple usage of your offering. Added value might lie in payments, service, financial structures, or the like.

In the case of the BioBarrier product, the team decided to do a competitive analysis with respect to these five links in a typical customers' experience: awareness, purchase, usage, service, and disposal. The team chose these five links because it felt that without having a solid advantage in these, it really wouldn't have a business at all. The reasoning was as follows:

- *Awareness:* Customers must become aware of the BioBarrier offer before they would even consider purchasing it.

- *Purchase:* Since most customers that the team envisioned for BioBarrier would be switching from some existing alternative, the team thought it must understand the switching risks from the customers' point of view and give some thought to reducing these risks.

- *Usage:* Obviously, the main selling point for a product like BioBarrier is that it delivers disinfection either more cost-effectively or with greater efficaciousness than do existing alternatives. Effectiveness is particularly important to some envisioned market segments, such as hospitals, because such customers would face legal liability if the product didn't work properly.

- *Service:* The team also believed that excellent service and immediate correction of any issues would be critical to maintaining customers' confidence. Since the product doesn't involve high switching costs, a bad experience with customer service could lose a customer for life.

- *Disposal:* Finally, since this sort of product is introduced into the customers' environment, whatever remains at the end of its usage needs to be thought through. If there are residues or remnants of the chemical after application, this could be a huge negative for customers.

NCO for BioBarrier in the Hospital Market

Table 5-5 compares the BioBarrier offering with the existing disinfecting solutions for the hospital market that the team had identified when they framed the venture. The five critical links are listed in the first column. The second and third columns list the NCO and BioBarrier attributes as they relate to each critical link. The final column shows the key differentiators that the team intended to deliver: namely, superior advertising exposure, a dedicated sales force with more sales calls per order, 50 percent better disinfection by the product, expedited overnight delivery for urgent orders, and no need to rinse off the used disinfectant. Note that the BioBarrier elected not to differentiate from, but to match, the NCO for all the other links in the consumption chain.

The NCO analysis basically lays out the key assumptions the team is making about where BioBarrier has a chance to establish a compelling

TABLE 5-5

Nearest competitor offering (NCO) analysis for BioBarrier

Consumption chain link	BioBarrier NCO	BioBarrier proposition	BioBarrier differentiator
Awareness	Product known	Heavy advertising	Advertising exposure
Purchase	Sales reps take orders	Dedicated sales force	Dedicated sales force
Usage	Surface/body application	Surface/body application	50% better disinfection
Service	Rapid delivery	Expedited overnight delivery	Expedited service
Disposal	Rinse after application	Key ingredient evaporates	No need to rinse

competitive advantage. Given the scope of the challenge the team will face (which we learned when doing the initial framing exercise), had the team not been able to come up with specific, actionable differentiators, we probably would have proposed killing the business. Since it does seem to be able to articulate a clear value proposition and why the business should win, the project continues to the next consideration, which is to look at the rest of the business model—what we call the key metrics that determine how likely the model is to work.

Key Metrics

When you have figured out how your offer might be better than a competing alternative, the last step in NCO analysis is to benchmark how you think your organization will do against the key metrics the competitive offer is already generating. You are looking for a point of clear difference that will be noticeable to target customers. If you don't have a point of major difference, and particularly if you don't think you will do as well on some measures that are important to customers, think carefully about your assumptions regarding why a customer would buy and what value you are adding.

Measures such as key performance indicators or value drivers represent the numbers that, given your business model and sources of advantage, influence important drivers of value creation. You want to understand the operational factors that will influence value creation, such as these:

- Sales growth

- Pricing strength as represented in margin growth

- Operating effectiveness

- Capital effectiveness

- Cost of capital[15]

Key metrics are used by executives to control their businesses (which are sometimes represented as operational dashboards that executives monitor), by analysts to estimate competitive effectiveness, and by investors to determine whether a company is a good or bad bet relative to competing alternatives.[16] Indeed, understanding the key metrics in a company is standard value investing practice.[17]

As a general rule, to the extent that your company outperforms competitors on one or more key metrics, you can gain a competitive advantage either by having a superior cost structure (as Dell did for years in computer distribution) or by having superior solutions for which customers will pay higher margins (as Nokia has long enjoyed in mobile telephony). In the case of the BioBarrier product, it's pretty clear that relative to the established industry, its costs for advertising, selling, and service are likely to be much higher than industry norm. For the project to be viable, these increased costs must be compensated for by additional margin, customer loyalty, or low operating costs.

Where Do Key Metrics Come From?

For most industries, the relevant key metrics develop because there is a resource that the business needs to leverage or that is directly correlated to sales growth. If we go back to the case of telephone-operating companies, the critical numbers for them measure how effectively they are selling minutes of time on a subscription basis. Thus, the industry has developed a measured called ARPU, or average revenue per user. Telephone-operating firms will subsidize phone subscriptions for the opportunity to increase their ARPU. This prompts them to negotiate with content providers (such as NBC and MTV) for the licensing rights to content that the operators hope will drive even more ARPU by giving customers a reason to spend time on the cell phone networks rather than on alternative sources of entertainment, communication, or information exchange.

By contrast, in the airline industry, a huge cost component lies in the relatively heavy fixed costs of purchasing and operating planes, reservation systems, and staff. How good the airline is at filling its planes also makes a difference, because unused seating capacity on a flight represents perishable revenues (and hence profits) that can never be recaptured. Consequently, two key metrics commonly used by airlines analysts are the fixed cost per passenger-mile flown and the passenger yield (meaning the extent to which the seats on the plane are filled).

Retailers operating conventional bricks-and-mortar stores have only so much floor space to use to display and sell items. For years, this space limitation has led analysts to use ratios such as same-store sales (in which sales for one period at one store are compared with a similar previous period) and sales per square foot (either compared with the stores' previous record or the performance of sister stores or competitors' stores). This is why we used the size of the store and the volume of toys that needed to be sold to make some judgments about the likely success of the toy store in chapter 1.

As a new player, if you are operating with the same unit of business that an established player uses, you had better be able to come up with some way of meeting most of the measures and exceeding some of them. Otherwise, what makes you think you are going to do any better than the industry average? If you are innovating with a new unit of business, you might speculate on how you would establish an advantage over the existing players at this point. The outcome of this part of the plan, therefore, is to specify the measures that you would like to meet in terms of competitive standard and that you need to beat.

If You Don't Know Your Current Key Metrics . . .

In a previous book, we suggested ways to identify your key metrics.[18] You can consult that list or visit www.discoverydrivengrowth.com, where we provide an exercise you can do to identify the key metrics that are most relevant to your industry.

A word of warning here that we cannot overemphasize: You do not need highly accurate data. You need plausible benchmarking data—plausible evidence that the metrics you are considering are in fact indicative of profits and profit growth and consistent with the way you are planning to differentiate your offering.

The point of a key metrics analysis is to estimate the impact of your business design on the customer experience you are seeking to create. What you are trying to establish is whether, relative to competing offerings, you can create a compelling set of attributes that enough customers will value. For instance, in "Shaking Up the Flower Business with a Different Business Model" (page 100), Proflowers' radical departure from existing norms in the flower business let it connect directly with customers, offer lower prices, and deliver fresher flowers. It's important to realize that key metrics on their own are not particularly important—it's what they ultimately do for customers that you want to understand.

In the next chapter, we show you how these assumptions get translated into operational numbers and linked to the plan's unfolding financials. We give some detailed examples using the BioBarrier model.

ACTION STEPS

1. Make sure you are clear on the corporate-level frame for a specific project, including necessary profits, revenue, and return on asset or investment specifications.

2. Now, start working on selecting a unit of business. Consider the needs that potential target customers are addressing by buying from you—try for a reasonably long list of possible needs. How are customers meeting those needs today? What are the drawbacks to the way the needs are addressed at the moment?

Question why the drawbacks exist—perhaps changes in technology, environment, or regulation have created the opportunity to serve customers in a different way without the negatives of the existing solutions.

3. Brainstorm—what are alternative ways (try to identify at least three) that you might charge a customer for something you can do? Some of the most common are these:

   - Charge for a physical unit (a toaster)

   - Charge for a service (a haircut or an outsourcing arrangement)

   - Sell a subscription (a magazine or a phone subscription)

   - Sell a specific outcome (an airplane trip)

   - Sell by time (consulting days)

   - Sell by assets used (computing power)

   - Sell by other resources used (office space or temporary help)

   - Sell by benefits (revenue-sharing or savings-capture arrangements)

   - Sell by creating benefits for end users or third parties (advertising, distribution, insurance through brokers)

4. Of these alternatives, are there any that eliminate the drawbacks of the existing approaches and create potential new positives for your target segments? If so, work with them to take the next step.

5. Guess what you could charge for your unit of business, by the time the project is mature.

6. Next, divide the required revenue by your unit price. How many units do you have to sell, according to this analysis?

7. Now do your NCO analysis and market size analysis. Do you have a clear point of differentiation? Will the market be big enough to sustain your business? Does it still look feasible?

8. If the plan is starting to look unrealistic, go back and rethink.

9. If it looks feasible at this stage, follow the steps in the next chapter.

CHAPTER SIX

Creating Reverse Financials and the Assumption Checklist

For each project that is going to make a contribution to the corporation's growth strategy, you have now thought through what the growth initiative needs to do to be successful: you've framed it. You've also defined a unit of business. You've compared your proposed offering with competitive alternatives and come up with at least one compelling point of differentiation. These form the basis for making some assumptions about the key metrics your organization will need to deliver to successfully create a differentiated customer experience. So far, the emphasis has been on evaluating proposed ideas—seeing if they make sense, being realistic about their limitations, and discarding ideas that don't seem to have strong potential. It is time to start learning more about what it will require to take the project from an idea to a real growth initiative.

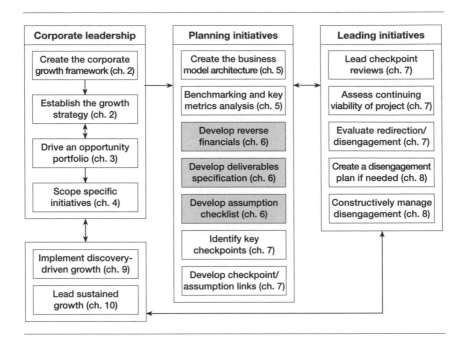

Corporate leadership	Planning initiatives	Leading initiatives
Create the corporate growth framework (ch. 2)	Create the business model architecture (ch. 5)	Lead checkpoint reviews (ch. 7)
Establish the growth strategy (ch. 2)	Benchmarking and key metrics analysis (ch. 5)	Assess continuing viability of project (ch. 7)
Drive an opportunity portfolio (ch. 3)	Develop reverse financials (ch. 6)	Evaluate redirection/ disengagement (ch. 7)
Scope specific initiatives (ch. 4)	Develop deliverables specification (ch. 6)	Create a disengagement plan if needed (ch. 8)
	Develop assumption checklist (ch. 6)	Constructively manage disengagement (ch. 8)
Implement discovery-driven growth (ch. 9)	Identify key checkpoints (ch. 7)	
Lead sustained growth (ch. 10)	Develop checkpoint/ assumption links (ch. 7)	

Fleshing Out Your Growth Project as a Plan to Learn

The next part of the process is to set up a plan to learn, which is different from a conventional plan. You'll develop several key documents to do this. First is a set of what we call *reverse financials*. These are financial documents (usually in spreadsheet form) that allow you to model how all the various assumptions in the initiative affect one another and whether, as you gain new information, the plan is getting traction or is at risk. The documents are intended to change as you learn, not to be a finished product. Second, we'll have a look at what we call the *deliverables specification*, which is a careful delineation of what needs to be accomplished in practice for the project to be successful. This includes things like the investment and activities required for marketing and selling, for service provision, for sourcing—in fact, for the delivery of all the links in your proposed customer consumption chain. Developed in parallel with the deliverables specification is an *assumption checklist*, which is what distinguishes discovery-driven planning from more conventional approaches. When you put all these together, you have assembled the blueprint for a well-designed experiment to test the assumptions in your hypothesized growth initiative. As it unfolds, the initiative will thus allow you to get closer and closer to your growth goals without imposing the unrealistic expectation of being right on the original plan. These steps are highlighted in our road map for the book.

Keep in mind that just because you have done a lot of work, this does not mean you are right. Many of the assumptions you have made so far are, in fact, almost certain to be wrong. That is actually just fine, because at this point, you haven't spent any real money, but have simply used some imagination to try to give direction and initial impetus to the nascent growth idea. Your goal going forward is to sharpen the focus of the project team so that you know more precisely what you need to learn before you do start spending any serious money.

A Simple Reverse Income Statement and an Example

As the name suggests, a *reverse,* or upside down, income statement starts with the bottom line and works backward into what the rest of the business must accomplish to deliver that bottom line, consistent with the idea of building the plan from the frame you established in chapter 4. It's a powerful tool that can help make sure your ideas are imbued with reality. All too often, companies simply don't do the disciplined thinking that forces them to articulate what must be accomplished. They assume "things will work themselves out because the opportunity is big" and end up with costly disappointments. For instance, a number of companies in the voice- and speech-recognition industries made the mistake of looking at rosy market size and growth numbers and projecting that all they needed was a tiny fraction of all that business. Most have foundered when their segment was slow to take off, and most applications haven't yet gone mainstream.

A favorite practice of our MBAs (real executives wouldn't do this, would they?) is to use spreadsheets to increment revenues, compounding each successive future year by 10 percent. Or saddest of all, some would-be venture folks let wishful thinking about issues such as size of the addressable market persuade them that the future is brighter than a more realistic view would suggest. The Segway PT human people transporter comes to mind—instead of the revolution that was hyped, it continues to be a niche application. Disappointed also were investors in nursing homes. Assuming that an aging population would lead to an explosion in the need for such services, investors had their hopes disappointed as the elderly found home-based alternatives more attractive and increasing life spans for both members of a married couple meant they could look after each other longer.

In developing a reverse income statement, you specify how much revenue is expected, how much cost is allowed to be incurred, what return on assets are necessary and therefore the maximum assets you can use in the endeavor, and how much you will be selling. The key difference in the discovery-driven approach is that because you have done this framing, you can be clear about what the project must accomplish if it is to be attractive.

Perhaps an example would help here. You're already familiar with G. Willikers, the toy shop whose hypothetical discovery-driven plan we introduced in chapter 1. The plan begins with the desired before-tax profit that we hypothesized our entrepreneur, Troy Carlsen, would like to earn from the venture: $250,000 per year. This exercise is analogous to the corporate-level frame we encourage people to develop, albeit in simple form. We hypothesized that his return on sales would be on the order of 50 percent, that his unit of business would be individual toys, and that the average price per toy would be $25. What this yields is an interesting number, the *allowable cost* figure. To develop the reverse income statement, we would make some guesses as to what the main processes in the business would require.

Note that in table 6-1 we begin the reverse income statement with a specification of profits from the business (before taxes) of $250,000 and a return on sales of 50 percent. This yields a required revenue number of $500,000 and an allowable-cost estimate of $250,000. In other words, provided that Carlsen can get the revenue to the $500,000 level while not spending more than $250,000 in costs, his plan has the potential to deliver the results he's looking for. In a discovery-driven plan, we would next work through the rest of the business activities required for success, beginning with the sales profile of the business. We assumed that the average price per item in his shop would be $25, which means he has to sell 20,000 items; and the average purchaser would buy 2 items, for an average number of sales of 10,000 in the year.

This calculation then naturally gives us a way to consider how to build up the consumption chain for the business. Before you can have sales, you need to build up awareness of your offer through advertising and marketing. Without knowing too much about the business, let's say that it will take $3 in expenses for each sale. At $3 times the 10,000 sales, that gives us an advertising and marketing budget of $30,000. Similarly, we'd need to think about costs for rent, inventory, and sales staff, as well as other expenses. We've noted those on the table, as well as how we got these figures—for the most part, these are just guesses we made. Working through the consumption chain for the business and comparing the costs to build it with the allowable-cost figure we estimated, we can see that if we are completely right (which we aren't), all Carlsen has left as a cost buffer before he starts eating into his required profits is $43,720. That money would have to cover any other expenses the business might incur. Again, the idea is to make the plan extremely grounded and practical, without obsessing over the details.

TABLE 6-1

Reverse income statement for toy business

Specification		Source
Required before-tax profits	$250,000	Management decision
Return on sales	50%	Assumption
Required revenues	$500,000	Calculation
Allowable costs	$250,000	Calculation
Unit of business	Per item	
Average price per item	$ 25	Assumption
Number of items required to be sold	20,000	Calculation
Average items per purchase	2	Assumption
Required purchases	10,000	Calculation
Advertising/marketing expense per sale	$ 3	Assumption
Total advertising/marketing expense	$ 30,000	Calculation
Rent on the shop per square foot	$ 30	Benchmark data
Size of shop in square feet	3,100	Actual data
Total rent	93,000	Calculation
Inventory costs per year as % of total sales	10%	Benchmark data
Total inventory costs	$ 50,000	Calculation
Sales staff expense per hour	$ 8	Benchmark data
Hours per week	40	Benchmark data
Sales staff expense per week	$ 320	Calculation
Weeks in the year	52	Actual data
Sales expense per year	$ 16,640	Calculation
Number of salespeople	2	Assumption
Sales expense per year	$ 33,280	Calculation
Allowable cost analysis		
Advertising/marketing expense	$ 30,000	From above
Rent	93,000	From above
Inventory costs	$ 50,000	From above
Sales expenses per year	$ 33,280	From above
Total anticipated costs	$206,280	Calculation
Allowable costs	$250,000	
Anticipated costs	$206,280	
Cost buffer	$ 43,720	Calculation

The Deliverables Specification

Just as we started with the required profits and revenue to get some idea of how big the nascent growth initiative has to be, now we're going to go through the rest of the financial statements, but upside down. We're going to take each set of activities that will be necessary to build a complete business and make some assumptions about how we'll do them, how much they will cost, and whether they are feasible.

From the reverse income statement, we can now begin to systematically work through the key metrics that you consider essential for delivering a customer experience superior to competitive offerings. You'll be working through the costs you will incur to deliver each link in particular customers' consumption chains and begin to subtract that cost from the allowable costs in the emerging income statement. In the same way, you can begin to decide which assets you must commit to deliver each link and begin to subtract that asset commitment from the allowable assets in the emerging balance sheet.

The process is to systematically develop each cost and asset requirement as you design the customers' experience, subtracting the associated cost and asset from those that you have allowed yourself in your earlier framing. To do this, you'll be concurrently developing another essential DDP tool, the *deliverables specification*.

Financial projections do not just happen—to get revenues and profits, someone has to sell something, produce and deliver it, incur costs, and acquire assets. The specification of these organizational deliverables creates the connection between your financials and the activities you will actually have to carry out to operate the growth initiative. The deliverables specification articulates your assumptions about the activities needed to create the desired customer experience.

Another major difference between a discovery-driven plan and a conventional one is that in a discovery-driven plan, you work backward into how the initiative must operate, given your requirements for profits and return on assets. For instance, the number of sales of units you need to close will dictate how many production lines you need to ship the required orders out of your plant. Or you might have to calculate how many consultant hours you must charge to generate enough consulting projects to produce the required consulting fees. Or you might calculate how many brokers you have to employ to sell enough insurance policies to generate your new stream of premiums. These numbers in turn will shape the costs incurred by the operational activities needed to deliver the key links in your customers' consumption chains.

There are four reasons why it is important to specify what the organization must be able to deliver in operational terms. First, it translates strategic directives into terms that everybody can understand. Specification of deliverables makes it clear to everyone how their specific activities map into the project and affect its performance. Second, deliverables specification provides a focus for competence creation. You need to specify what must be done to make the financial numbers happen. Third, it is in the operation of a business that many of the most dangerous assumptions reside. For instance, we have seen many otherwise insightful venture managers gaily assume that the incumbent sales force will be delighted to have their spanking-new offering to sell. Not so. Most of the time, the salespeople would rather go on selling products they already know and whose quirks they have worked out for commissions on sales to customers who almost automatically place orders rather than have to be sold. Even taking the time to learn about your product is time spent not selling. Finally, the richer and more integrated the activities included in your set of deliverables are, the harder it is for a competitor to come along and copy them. So if your bank account offering includes investment advice, access to product discounts from vendors, automatic access to overseas financial institutions, and credit card and debit card services, your competitors will have to assemble similar capabilities to match yours before they can copy you.

In a working session (ideally populated with people who each have a different functional perspective—especially marketing, sales, finance, and operations—plus people with some actual knowledge of how things work in the target industry) for a typical manufacturing project, you would go through questions like these:

- How many salespeople need to make how many sales calls with what kind of hit rate to get the orders needed to generate the projected revenues?

- What percentage of revenues need to be spent on advertising to create awareness that our offering exists in the target segment? What percentage of those that are made aware of our services will become customers?

- How many deliveries need to be made by what number of orders per delivery to meet the orders that will generate revenues?

And so on.

On the other hand, for a typical Internet-based business, you would work through questions like these:

- How many clicks must be recorded by what percentage of site visitors to generate the advertising revenues we need?

- How many complaints or returns per order will we have to process?

- How many help desk calls per customer will we have handle, and for how long?

- How many fraudulent claims will we have to process per guarantee, policy, or service agreement?

- How many people will we need in the back office to support the operating system?

The questions are illustrative—each project will have its own set of appropriate questions relevant to its consumption chain.

As you can see, for each business design, people will make specific assumptions about how the business will operate. The goal is not to be precise or to be perfect. If you're just getting started, the goal is to make sure that you are not setting yourself up to fail by building unrealistic operating assumptions into your plan or by neglecting a major cost or asset commitment that is going to be needed to deliver the business (see "Catching Dangerous Assumptions—Before They Can Hurt You!").

Catching Dangerous Assumptions— Before They Can Hurt You!

An example of how business leaders can create unrealistic plans (even with very good intentions) emerged during one of our DDP workshops. As we were working through the deliverables specification, the senior team leader mentioned that he had agreed with his boss that the goal for the venture would be to start generating cash flow within twelve months. We noticed that in the deliverables specification, the plan was not to use the existing company sales force, but to recruit an entirely new sales force (because the target customer was at a different organizational level and had an entirely different set of needs than the existing business did).

Making this assumption explicit triggered some concerns among the planning group. Though the executive was looking for cash within twelve months from a new offer, he did not yet have a single person in sales. Well, logically, the question was, how long will it take to recruit even one really good salesperson, let alone a new team? Let's be generous and say it would take four months (if he started recruiting immediately). That

The Assumption Checklist

In chapter 1, we argued that as a main benefit, discovery-driven planning helps you overcome a host of cognitive and emotional biases that tend to get in the way of your making the right decisions with respect to new businesses. The assumption checklist is key to effectively handling situations with what we call a high assumption-to-knowledge ratio. It requires you to make assumptions explicit and therefore makes them visible. It forces you to share them with others who can weigh in, which makes them less vulnerable to just one person's point

---

leaves eight months to generate cash. How long before the brand-new salesperson learns enough about the product or service offering to communicate it effectively? Say another four months. That leaves just four months to create awareness, make customer calls, consummate the deal, and have cash coming in the door. And this for the sale of a brand-new offering that customers are unfamiliar with? We don't think so . . .

This discussion prompted a major rethink of the planned approach to entering the market. The team came up with a different idea, namely, to develop the offering jointly with a pilot customer. The "sell" in this case was probably from the senior team leader to his senior peers in the customer company. Best of all, engaging the customer early enough was almost certain to result in a better design and a more robust offering for everyone.

As it turned out, this approach worked very well. The senior peer, in fact, was so satisfied that the entire pilot customer organization became evangelists within their industry for the new product, which rapidly produced a hefty cash flow with virtually no sales staff on board.

This illustrates one of our major themes: using DDP can help you pinpoint places where you *really* need to be creative as well as avoid a lot of the potential pain in the innovative process.

---

of view. And because they are explicitly flagged as assumptions, there is less incentive to defend them to the death in an effort to be right.

The assumption checklist is a companion document to the deliverables specification. It is intended to provide a summary of the key assumptions that you are making as you go through thinking about project deliverables. Different projects will capture different assumptions in their checklists. Table 6-2 is a template for one that we often use as a starting point.

The "Assumption Description" column is narrative; it describes what you are assuming—for instance, product price, number of salespeople, or salary of production worker. It behooves you to focus on the most critical assumptions, which are generally associated with your key consumption-chain links. Otherwise, you will find your team submerged and overwhelmed by too many detailed assumptions with which you can be very wrong and affect the outcome very little. Especially in the early stages of a project, you should avoid getting into too much detail—you are going to be wrong, anyway, and replanning is more painful the more detailed the planning. To start, you can often use industry ratios from the industry you are entering as broad indicators of key cost and asset requirements, as we did in the toy store case.

TABLE 6-2

Sample assumption checklist

Assumption number	Assumption description	Relevant data	Source	Date last checked	Responsible party	Notes

Some Typical Critical Assumptions

Although every business is different, here are some typical assumptions that can end up being critical for the project. Note that no assumption in this list is critical for every growth project.

Assumptions About the Business Model

- Cost, asset, revenue architectures, and timing

- Major obstacles and feasibility of breaking through them

Assumptions About the Market

- Who will buy and why: quantity, continuity, and frequency

- How the different market segments will behave

- Market growth rate

- Cost and time to achieve target volume or share

- Distribution channels and access to them

- Price, product, functionality, service, marketing strategy

Assumptions About Developing the Product or Service

- Development time and cost

- Functional characteristics related to market need

Assumptions About Competition

- Advantage compared with competitive products

- Duration of product advantages

- Type of competition that will be faced

- Likely competitive response

Assumptions About Manufacturing and Production

- Ability to control product costs and quality

- Service requirements and costs

- Ability to produce at required scale

- Availability of people with required knowledge and skills

Financial Assumptions

- Development time and cost

- Cash required to reach cash breakeven

- Daily, weekly, monthly breakevens

- Breakdown of the numbers into actionable pieces

- Investment required for profit-and-loss breakeven, to reach profit objectives

- Gross and net margins

- Time required to achieve above

- Costs, profit and loss, at varying volume levels

The "Relevant Data" column in table 6-2 is where you would put your current best estimate. So, for instance, if you believe that your gross margin is going to be 45 percent, you'd write "gross margin" in the first column and "45 percent" in the second column.

The "Source" column asks you where the assumption came from. Was it a consulting report? A market trial? Competitive intelligence? The reason this is such an important thing to document is that assumptions can often get baked into plans, even when they are based on the flimsiest of evidence. It's also important to remember that in a situation of real uncertainty, nobody can accurately predict the future. Just because the Gartner Group said it, doesn't mean it's a fact—it means that some smart, highly educated people have made a conjecture.

The "Date Last Checked" column helps you avoid leaving important assumptions go untested in your plan. Unless it's the kind of assumption that has a yes-or-no answer, most assumptions should be checked at regular intervals. The "Responsible Party" column typically refers to the person who has agreed to follow up on the assumption or who has the most information about it. In some companies, one person takes on the onus of monitoring assumptions (in an earlier article, we called this person the "keeper of the assumptions"). In other firms, the responsibility is dispersed. In any case, you want to know who the best source for information about an assumption is—don't leave it in a vacuum.

The assumption number will help members of the team connect the assumption checklist and your overall plan. And of course, notes are helpful for recording stuff that doesn't have a column.

Don't Be Obsessive, but Do Get Feedback

As you develop your deliverables specification, it is important to make a trade-off between superficiality and obsession with detail. We like to start with a rough-hewn plan that acts as a straw person. You are after a point of departure for the vigorous conversation and debate that are essential to the discipline of DDP. At this point, your deliverables assumption doesn't need to be completely accurate or even wholly complete. (Remember, under uncertain conditions, roughly right is better than precisely wrong!) You need to aggressively use your discovery-driven plan to elicit questions and feedback and to get people thinking.

The folks working with you (usually the venture team) can use the discovery-driven plan to elicit information from people knowledgeable about similar markets, technologies, operations, distribution, and logistics. Ask people to weigh in on how reasonable the assumptions in the initial plan are. If they express concern, find out why. Ask them for their best alternative number and their reasoning. If they raise additional considerations, make a note of them in your assumptions checklist. Often, a few phone calls or a conversation with an acquaintance, an industry expert, a potential customer, a supplier, or a distributor can uncover a massive amount of information.

You can build a bottom-up specification of organizational deliverables on a simple spreadsheet without spending any money at all. Flaws and unwarranted assumptions often become glaringly obvious, affording you the luxury of being totally wrong without having to pay the price of failure. Again, using DDP can create a far less painful innovation process than trying to fit uncertain projects into plans intended for operations that are more definite.

Summary of Steps in Creating the Reverse Financials

Now that you better understand the components of the reverse financials, you can follow these steps to create an actual reverse financial analysis.

Step 1: Develop a reverse income statement. This is going to let you know how many units you need to sell and, just as importantly, the maximum cost you can incur to meet your profit and profitability numbers. It's also going to give you an idea of the required scope of your growth initiative, which will have implications for what you need to do in terms of marketing, selling, production, information technology, and other costs.

Step 2: Develop the deliverables specification. This document lays out how you think you are going to create a complete offering from a customer point of view. We often couch it in terms of how you will address each important link in the customers' consumption chain. As you do this, you'll be making quite a few assumptions. The ones we are most interested in at the moment are the ones that will affect expenditures and asset commitments. You'll be subtracting the expenses and asset commitments from the "allowable" sections in your reverse income statement and reverse balance sheet.

Most of the time, you'll be doing your deliverables specification using a spreadsheet or specialized planning software. You'll want to do several things that make the spreadsheet manageable and relevant:

- Place a row number for each relevant data point in your plan.

- Record the relevant data (costs or revenue amounts).

- Define the type of information in the row. We flag whether a particular bit of information is based on an assumption, a management specification, or a calculation using other numbers in the plan. We find it helpful to highlight critical assumptions (we use green) so that you can immediately see where the assumptions in the plan are.

- You may like to put benchmark data in the plan as well, in order to remember why certain critical decisions were made. In this case, you would have one column for the benchmark and one for the plan.

- You'll also want to include notes on where the number came from, particularly if it is a calculation.

- Finally, if the number is an assumption, you will find it helpful to give each assumption a unique number. This will be useful later on, when we try to understand the connection between major events in the life of the venture and the testing of assumptions.

Step 3: Occurring in parallel with step 2, this is to begin developing the assumption checklist. As we've described, the checklist summarizes the key assumptions you are making, why you believed them to be reasonable at the time you made them, and where they came from. We also recommend that you note the last time you checked a critical assumption, just to make sure you haven't overlooked anything important.

Step 4: Using the same bottom-up idea, you can now develop a reverse balance sheet showing the maximum assets you can deploy and still make your return targets, plus the major assets you will be needing to operate the initiative. You will also see how much of a cost cushion you have without your costs starting to infringe on your desired profit outcomes.

Step 5: Having thought all this through, take the final step, analysis, to try to grasp the implications. This is best done with a team that can bring diverse perspectives to the analysis. As you think through the plan that is unfolding, you'll be challenging its basic structure. Are you going to be able to run the growth initiative within the allowed cost structure? Are you being realistic about the time estimates? If the project is very expensive or very risky, you may wish to do some simple modeling to see how sensitive the plan is to variations in assumptions. We'll get to some of those details toward the end of the chapter.

A BioBarrier Example

Recall that we are assuming that the BioBarrier project is a growth initiative focused on building a new business whose key point of differentiation is that it is a supereffective disinfectant that will be much more cost effective for use in hospitals than competing alternatives. For the project to make financial sense for MC Chem, the parent company, we concluded that the venture would have to generate at least $50 million in revenue (chapter 4). When the team considered the unit of business for the product, it concluded that there was no particular benefit to changing the unit that was then prevalent in the disinfecting business, a gallon of fluid (chapter 5). As you may remember, the team was pinning its hopes for selling the product on the idea that BioBarrier could undercut prevalent pricing in the industry by 10 percent and sell a gallon for $50. This implies annual sales of one million gallons when the new business is mature. By the way, we don't necessarily agree with this pricing approach—if you are adding more value, you should be charging for it at the outset, as it is usually hard to raise prices once you are in the market.

Putting It All Together: From Initial Frame to Reverse Financials and Deliverables Specification

In chapter 4, we developed for the BioBarrier project a frame that is consistent with these numbers. The initial frame now becomes the beginning of your reverse income statement and deliverables specification when operational information is added to the numbers in the original table. We've set up table 6-3 to be consistent with the fields we would use for a spreadsheet or project plan. Note that we've flagged the pricing assumption of $50 as an assumption (row F7). Note also that this table establishes the upper bounds of what we can spend to create the deliverables in the initiative by specifying that we can spend no more than $40 million to operate the growth initiative (row F6).

With this statement set up, we can now begin to see how the new business would actually deliver the customer experience we designed in chapter 5. You'll recall that a major differentiator for BioBarrier is that the "awareness" and "purchase" links of the chain would be characterized by heavy advertising and a dedicated, technically savvy sales force. We'll next determine the specific key metrics that would characterize the difference between industry norm and our plans for BioBarrier. We would then translate these metrics into assumptions and calculations to see if meeting the plan is actually feasible. Table 6-4 shows you how this translation might look on a spreadsheet.

Research done by the team suggested that industry average spending by competitive firms on advertising (as a percentage of sales) is about 6 percent (row F29). The team assumed that to have an appreciably significant effect on customer awareness, the project needed to

TABLE 6-3

Beginning of BioBarrier reverse income statement

Row no.	Data	Basis	Benchmark	Our plan	Source or formula	Assumption no.
F1	Operating profit	Management decision		$10,000,000		
F2	Required ROA	Management decision	20%	33.3%		
F3	Required margin	Management decision	15%	20%		
F4	Allowable assets	Calculation		$30,030,030	F1/F2	
F5	Necessary revenues	Calculation		$50,000,000	F1/F3	
F6	Allowable costs	Calculation		$40,000,000	F5 – F1	
F7	Selling price per gallon	Assumption: 10% less than NCO	$55 current competitive price	$50		1
F8	Required gallons of sales	Calculation		1,000,000	F5/F7	
F9	Gallons per day (250-day year)	Calculation		4,000	F8/250	

ROA, return on assets; NCO, nearest competitive offering.

be prepared to spend double the industry average, or 12 percent, on advertising. Further, the team assumed that the salespeople would need to make more sales calls than they would for the standard product, yet fewer sales calls in one day than for existing standard products. These salespeople, because they were expected to operate at a higher level than the level of standard salespeople, would expect to be paid a more generous commission. For our hypothetical example, the team was planning to pay 15 percent as opposed to the industry norm of 10 percent commission. As each of these data points and assumptions are articulated, they can go into the plan.

This analysis suggests several conclusions. First, if we are genuinely going to build a differentiated awareness and purchase experience,

TABLE 6-4

Spreadsheet for superior awareness and purchase experience

Row no.	Data	Basis	Benchmark	Our plan	Source or formula	Assump- tion no.
F29	Advertising as % of sales	Industry average	6%	12%	Industry association report	2
F30	Total ad spending	Calculation	$6,000,000		F21 × F29	
F32	Gallons per order	Assumption	10	10	Distributors	3
F33	Sales calls per order	Assumption	2	5	Distributors	4
F34	Sales calls per day	Assumption	8	6	Distributors	5
F35	Sales days per year	Assumption	250	250	Distributors	6
F36	Gallons per salesperson per year	Calculation		3,000	F32 × F34/ F33 × F35	
F37	Salesforce required	Calculation		333	F25/F36	
F38	Sales commission	Assumption	10%	15%	Competitors	7
F39	Sales salary	Assumption	$30,000	$30,000	Competitors	8
F40	Total commissions	Calculation	$7,500,000		F21 × F38	
F41	Total salaries	Calculation	$10,000,000		F37 × F39	
F42	Total selling cost	Calculation	$17,500,000		F40 + F41	

we're going to have to be able to afford a much more intensive and expensive selling process. Second, the scope of the new initiative is quite substantial, requiring 333 salespeople (F37), with each salesperson having to move 3,000 gallons of the BioBarrier fluid per year (F36).

There are no hard-and-fast rules about which assumptions you choose to emphasize—part of the skill of doing a discovery-driven plan is figuring out the rhythm of different businesses. For instance, in the case of BioBarrier, we are assuming a business that is more or less constant throughout the year. In the toy store example from chapter 1, we assumed that business was highly cyclical and added the relevant assumptions for that model.

To develop a complete reverse income statement, you would work through the rest of the key metrics necessary to deliver the consumption chain we specified. These metrics would include how the manufacturing and distribution processes would work, what assets we would need to support the business, and assumptions about issues such as overhead costs. In the interest of brevity, we won't go through all that here. The complete BioBarrier reverse income statement spreadsheet is available at www.discoverydrivengrowth.com if you would like to download it.

Probing for Feasibility

As you complete each component of the deliverables specification, you'll be spelling out your best-guess assumptions for the key metrics that will underpin the business. These can now be put together in a more developed reverse income statement, which summarizes the costs to deliver the key metrics, numbers you can compare with the business frame you set up in chapter 2. Table 6-5 summarizes such an analysis for the BioBarrier business (first cut). You add up all the costs that will be necessary to deliver the business, and then you see whether you can meet the maximum parameters you established in the frame.

This model reveals several disturbing relationships about the parameters of the BioBarrier business and our discovery-driven frame. First, if the deliverables specification works out as we expect, costs will be higher and profits lower than specified by management in the frame. This calls into question the original justification for the growth initiative, namely, that it will allow MC Chem to enter markets that are more attractive than its existing core business. Second, the initiative

TABLE 6-5

Reverse income statement after deliverables development

Plan element	Data	Comments
Required revenue	$50,000,000	From original frame
Total allowable costs	$40,000,000	From original frame
Selling costs	$17,500,000	From table 6-4, row F42
Advertising costs	$ 6,000,000	Assumption
Materials costs	$13,000,000	Calculated
Production salaries	$ 1,680,000	Calculated
Delivery costs	$ 400,000	Calculated
Depreciation charges	$ 1,200,000	Calculated
Overheads	$ 5,000,000	Calculated
Total of all cost elements	$44,780,000	
Excess costs	$ 4,780,000	
Total anticipated profit	$ 5,220,000	Instead of required $10M
Return on sales	10.4%	Instead of required 20%

turns out to be extremely sales and marketing intensive, if BioBarrier is be able to unseat established methods at a more competitive price. You can use the elements from the reverse income statement to finish the relevant assumption checklist for the project, as we show in table 6-6.

The reverse income statement in table 6-5 suggests that the plan, as it's been conceived at the moment, is not going to work out as the Bio-Barrier team had hoped. That's not necessarily bad news. Remember, we haven't spent any money yet! The question is whether we can conceive of a way of doing the business differently, so that a more attractive plan can be conceived, or whether we would be better off thinking of a different approach to commercializing the underlying technology of BioBarrier. The project might benefit by being creatively redirected to a different model, a different target market, or a different application. This is a very normal part of discovery-driven planning. It is also a hugely valuable part of the process—it allows your company to

TABLE 6-6

Assumption checklist for BioBarrier, first three assumptions

Assumption description	Relevant data	Source	Date last checked	Responsible party	Assumption number	Notes
Selling price per gallon	10% less than NCO, or $50	Current price at $55	7/6/2008	Head of marketing	1	
Advertising expense as a % of sales	Double industry average, or $6 million, given projected size of business	Industry is 6%, according to analyst; given need to create awareness, we'll need to spend more	5/4/2008	Head of marketing	2	Ad effectiveness will be a crucial determinant of success
Gallons per order	Assume 10	Distributors say this is the current amount	5/5/2008	Head of operations	3	
And so on . . .						

rapidly and cheaply identify whether a proposed growth initiative will have traction. In this way, it allows your firm to efficiently set aside and avoid expensive proposals that do not have traction and focus funds and more important creative talent on the fewer projects that do have brighter growth prospects. At this point, the BioBarrier team needs to find a way of redirecting the strategy or must turn to better opportunities.

What you should have by now in your planning process is an initial set of reverse financials, an early-stage deliverables specification that lays out your assumptions regarding how the growth initiative will operate, and the initial assumption checklist that collects all your assumptions in one place. Most of the time, this will be enough to go on to the next step. Sometimes, however, for a very complex, risky, or expensive project, it is worth doing analyses that are a little more sophisticated than what we've done so far.

More Sophisticated Analyses

So far, we have talked about the elements that make up the deliverables specification in terms of single-point estimates. We all know that life is far messier than that. One way to add an additional level of sophistication to your analysis is to specify ranges for the assumptions you are making. If you have absolutely no idea, you'd specify a very wide range. If you are pretty sure you're within a percentage, you would specify a much narrower range. In the BioBarrier case, for example, you might specify a range of possible prices that goes way under $50 or way over it.

Once you have specified the ranges for the major assumptions in your plan, you can use that data as input to a simulation program. All a simulation does is calculate the outcomes of your plan over and over again with different values selected from the ranges of your inputs. It's just a fast way of doing a what-if with your spreadsheet hundreds of times. The simulation gives you a picture of what would happen if the business were started for real and it ran those numbers hundreds of times, each time experiencing your input variables (your assumptions) at a specific value in the range that you gave it. You can then tell the simulation program to analyze which of the input variables have the greatest impact on outcomes such as revenue or profit, so that you can focus your creativity on the highest-impact elements of the different assumptions in your plan. Such an analysis can tell you which assumptions are the most significant to your bottom-line results and which don't really matter.

On the Web site for this book (www.discoverydrivengrowth.com), you can download a simple, easy-to-use software package we have developed that lets you run simple simulations for your plan. Among the outputs of the package is a staircase chart, which visually shows you which assumptions make a really big difference and which ones don't.

For the hypothetical BioBarrier business, the staircase chart is shown in figure 6-1.

Note that only a few assumptions have a major impact on profits for BioBarrier: gallons per order, selling price per gallon, sales calls per day, and sales calls per order are far more important than most of the other variables. This reflects the strategy of the team—to differentiate BioBarrier by a massive focus on the purchasing link.

FIGURE 6-1

The most sensitive assumptions for profits

This staircase chart illustrates sensitivity. It shows the contribution to the upside and downside of the output variable, as the input varies from a middle value to a maximum and a minimum.

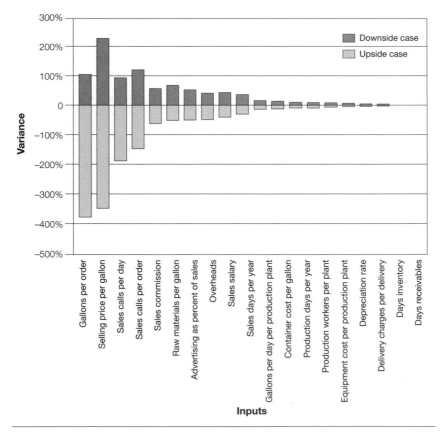

For your top-sensitivity assumptions, it behooves you to find several ways to revisit these assumptions as the project unfolds. Moreover, you should find creative ways to test these particular assumptions as early and cheaply as possible. If the impact of these variables does not rapidly diminish as the plan unfolds, you are not learning and need to seriously consider disbanding the project.

Another output you can get from a simulation program is a picture of the probability distribution of costs and revenue. For instance, the simulation of BioBarrier yielded a frequency chart shown by figure 6-2.

You can see that while BioBarrier has an expected profit of no less than $3.7 million per year, if we have bad luck and all the worst assumptions happen, BioBarrier will lose as much as $14.3 million per year, while if all goes well it will harvest $11.7 million dollars per year. The challenge for the team is to find ways of checking along the way to ensure that if the left tail starts to dominate, the team can cut its losses. This leads to the need for checkpoints to test assumptions, which is the topic of the next chapter.

FIGURE 6-2

Distribution of profits at BioBarrier

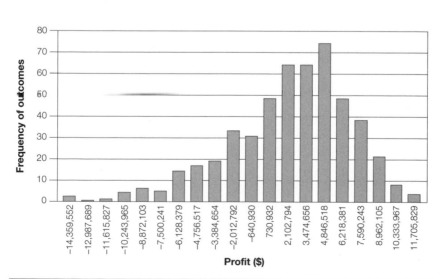

ACTION STEPS

1. Following the instructions in this chapter, develop the reverse financial statements—specify the performance of the income statement and balance sheet for the project at maturity, or at steady-state conditions.

2. Develop the initial deliverables specification, and as you are doing that, fill in the assumption checklist.

3. Consider whether, given the assumptions you are working with, the growth initiative still looks viable. Does the project avoid eating into your allowable costs, and can it deliver your required profits? Think about what might happen if a few of the more important assumptions were wrong (for instance, if price were 10 percent below what you expected, or volumes were smaller, or costs much higher).

4. If you have the appetite, do a few of the more sophisticated analyses and think over the implications.

5. If the growth initiative doesn't look viable, creatively consider what might need to be done to improve it—sell at higher price? Reduce costs? Scale down? Different target market? Different offer? Joint venture?

6. For the projects that look viable, move on to the next chapter.

CHAPTER SEVEN

Actively Managing and Redirecting Projects

At this point in the development of your project, you will have built a base business case from which you will be deriving your plan to learn. In this chapter, we'll take you through the last tool that you'll be working with in setting up the plan: the checkpoint review chart. We'll also show you how the assumption checklist from chapter 6 and the checkpoint review chart work together as your plan goes forward. The power of discovery-driven planning, however, does not lie in the plan documents. It lies in the way you use them to engage every member of your team—and other knowledgeable people—to learn their way to the true growth opportunity or to avoid painful missteps early on.

Essentially, in this chapter, we'll cover the transition from planning an initiative to leading it, integrating the planning steps with how you

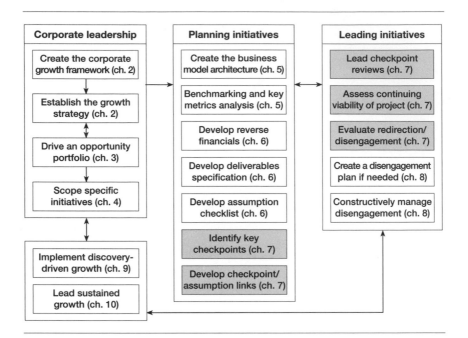

use them to lead a venture. These activities are shaded on our road map for the book.

Using Checkpoints

In any emerging business, you will learn a lot from situations that reveal how close your assumptions are to what is actually unfolding. Sometimes, these situations or events occur naturally as you work on developing the business: a prospective customer might give you information about what value he or she would have for a given solution, or one of your researchers might have a breakthrough idea for solving a technical problem. Other times, you'll have to deliberately create a management intervention to get at the information—such as doing a pilot study or building a prototype system. We can use these events as checkpoints in the discovery-driven plan to deliberately structure the systematic testing of assumptions as the plan unfolds. So the next big planning activity is to design a set of checkpoints to monitor, manage, and redirect the progress of the plan.

A Different Review Rhythm and Management Structure Needed for Uncertain Growth Projects

Time and business dynamics exert a certain tyranny on business: everybody runs around like crazy as the peak seasons in the fiscal year descend upon them; people attempt to make decisions fit neatly into a given planning horizon. The dilemma with such calendar-oriented review cycles is that they can waste a lot of everyone's time on pointless preparation and discussion if the review of progress is done too early, and a company can miss the opportunity to save costs or redirect if the review is done too late.

What we suggest instead is to create review rhythms that reflect the underlying dynamics of the growth initiative itself.[1] Project reviews happen when enough learning and development activity has been completed that a review makes sense, or when a significant decision to invest in, reorient, or shut the business needs to be made.

At Nokia, reviews are pegged to the resource intensity of the project, which are called *V milestones*. This practice further reduces risks. As a manager described it:

VO is the stage where we have recognized the business idea, have the critical elements of the business idea, let's say target customer group, the product concept, the need of the target group we are trying to fulfill, the benefit our apparatus is giving them and the position in competition. We also must have recognized the upside potential for the idea in a corporate scale and also in financial terms . . . At V1 we could have some kind of pilot, depending on what kind of business model we are talking about; we could have the first test if the idea works with some representative customers . . . if partners are needed, we would have some partners; if technology is needed [at this stage], it is tested or demonstrated, verified. V2 would be the market or business commitment phase . . . V3 would be [the stage] where a traditional VC exits, when it is a full blown business.[2]

When you get to a critical checkpoint, you have a lot of choices to make rather than just blindly continuing: you can stop the project, change its direction, break it apart in some way, spin it off, put it on hold, fold it into another business, or move it more aggressively to launch. We find that project managers are often so fixed on a single outcome for their initiative that an outside perspective may be necessary if a project team is to seriously consider these alternatives.

Checkpoints and Redirection Go Together

Checkpoint-based planning differs from conventional approaches. First, it differs from processes like stage-gate planning in that it drives the plan by key learning events, rather than preconceived stages. Indeed, recent research suggests that stage-gate processes are often dangerous to innovative processes and inhibit learning.[3] Second, checkpoint planning encourages the consideration of far more options for the venture than just plain go/no-go. Third, checkpoint planning follows a unique schedule, unlike the more common calendar-based planning, in which projects are budgeted and reviewed on a predetermined calendar basis, regardless of critical developments in the growth project.

Checkpoint planning is consistent with the idea of treating ventures as options. If a project is revealed to be infeasible, the decision gets made with a more modest loss than if a more expensive checkpoint were put first. By moving checkpoints that can be reached cheaply to an earlier point in the plan and by postponing those that will require significant investment, you can often save yourself a lot of unnecessary expense by redirecting your activities early on. The box "Creating a Low-Cost, Low-Risk Checkpoint" gives a good example of just how one company did this with low risk and low cost. The experience of Air Products and Chemicals, Inc., a firm that has adopted discovery-driven planning, shows how this can work.

Creating a Low-Cost, Low-Risk Checkpoint

One growth project we helped plan involved a company's proposal to build a plant in mainland China to deliver top-quality products to industrial customers. Two of the key assumptions in the plan were that top quality would be appreciated by Chinese firms and that our client firm could get prices similar to those that U.S.-based firms were paying.

We suggested that the firm create a checkpoint to test pricing assumptions. In this case, it was a mock sales pitch that was proposed to potential customers before the company was ready to offer its product. The assumption about pricing was found to be completely wrong. The majority of the Chinese firms pitched were interested only in reasonable quality, at cutthroat prices. Our client would never be able to make money, given its cost structure.

The company decided instead to redirect the project. It found that there were many local producers selling low-cost, low-quality commodity products. Instead of building a full-scale plant to produce product from scratch, the firm installed a low-cost plant that purchased local product and then upgraded its quality, buying the low-quality product from local producers eager to off-load capacity at rock-bottom prices and selling to the minority of customers that were more quality sensitive. The venture has delivered very satisfying growth and profitability and, more importantly, established our client's reputation as a reputable quality producer in the Chinese market.

Two members of the venture team were a division head, who was looking to introduce a new product, and Ron Pierantozzi, the former new business development director. On one of their ventures, the division head proposed to conduct technological testing as a first milestone (based on the logic that if the technology didn't work, they wouldn't have a venture). Pierantozzi proposed instead that they conduct a preliminary market-needs review (a far faster and less expensive activity) on the opposing assumption that if the market need didn't exist, it didn't matter how good the technology was.

Pierantozzi prevailed. The market assessment revealed that the customers' actual problem would need a somewhat different technical solution. Given the insights from the market study, we can see that had they done the proposed technical testing first, the testing would have had to be redone, almost doubling the cost of the venture. In this case, the venture was redirected from one customer solution to another at an early stage.

Identifying Checkpoints

You can develop a list of checkpoints with the same reverse thinking that we've been using throughout this book. First, consider your grown-up initiative at steady state. Next, think about all the major events that must occur for this steady-state condition to take place. You can also consider events that are likely to occur, even if you are not the one making them happen (such as competitive response or customer returns). You can use the list in table 7-1 to trigger your creativity, but please add your own checkpoint specific to the project.

Different types of businesses will have different checkpoints that matter specifically to them. In table 7-1, we contrast typical checkpoints that are usually relevant to a new manufacturing type business with those for a service business.

As ever, try not to obsess here. In the early stages, five to ten checkpoints should be ample. As your costs and investments increase, you

TABLE 7-1

Typical checkpoint events

Manufacturing project	Service project
Market study	Market study
Industry analysis	Industry analysis
Feasibility study	Feasibility study
Development of prototype	Development of mock-up system
Initial customer test with focus groups	Initial customer test with focus groups
Human resource and manpower study	Human resource and manpower study
Market research: conjoint analyses	Market research: conjoint analyses
Trials with beta users	Trials with beta users
Focus group discussions with beta users	Trials with beta users
Pilot plant	Pilot system development
Pilot marketing campaign	Pilot marketing campaign
Plant design and site acquisition	Test operating system development
Pilot sales recruitment and training	Pilot sales recruitment and training
Plant construction launch line 1	System testing with beta users
Manufacturing recruitment and training	Operations staff recruitment and training
Plant commissioning	Call center recruitment and training
Sales recruitment and training	Sales recruitment and training
Product launch	Service product launch
Full-scale plant construction launch	Full-scale system launch

may need to add more checkpoints, but try to keep it under twenty. Remember, you are likely to have to redirect and therefore replan as the project develops, so too much effort on distant checkpoints will both waste energy and discourage replanning! More checkpoints can always be added as the project develops—it is the early ones that really matter at the beginning.

The Initial Checkpoint/Assumption Chart

At this point in the planning process, we start bringing the whole thing together. Go back to your assumption checklist from chapter 6. You are now going to link the assumptions and the checkpoints. The goal is to have a chart that will help you identify which assumptions will be tested at which checkpoint—bearing in mind that many assumptions, particularly the most critical assumptions, might be tested more than once. We like to plot the chart with the assumptions down the side and the major checkpoints across the top, as in table 7-2. Note that we have flagged when a particular assumption will be tested—at which milestone—with a check mark.

A few things about the table bear special mention. First, note that some assumptions (such as number 4) get tested frequently, indeed, virtually at every checkpoint. Price and competitive behavior would be examples of assumptions you need to revisit every time. Second, note that some assumptions get tested once or only a few times—these are typically assumptions with a yes-or-no answer or assumptions that simply require data for you to be able to draw a conclusion. The golden rule is never to have an assumption in your plan without at least one corresponding checkpoint. If you have an empty row, you need to think of a creative way to generate a checkpoint to test the assumption. Nor should there ever be a checkpoint column that does not test some assumption—it is a lost opportunity to do some validation.

Self-created checkpoints are necessary when there isn't a natural event for testing assumptions, but when there are major uncertainties

TABLE 7-2

Initial checkpoint/assumption chart

| | CHECKPOINTS | | | | | | |
Assumption	1	2	3	4	5	6	7
1	✔	✔					
2			✔				
3	✔			✔	✔		
4	✔	✔	✔	✔	✔	✔	✔
5		✔		✔			

that could be expensive if your assumptions are wrong. In software, for instance, if you were testing user reaction to an interface, it would be far less expensive to put users in front of a user-interface prototype that has little functionality than it would be to fully program the software and have to come back later. If you can put a device (even if it doesn't fully work) in someone's hand, you will often get far more relevant feedback early on than if you are working with verbal descriptions.[4] And a mocked-up environment can often teach you a lot without your having to risk the unexpected in reality. One of the more interesting recent developments in the world of prototyping and market testing is the use of virtual worlds, such as the online game Second Life, to test potential customers' reactions.

As you go through your actual planning process, you may find that the connection between checkpoints and assumptions can be more conveniently laid out in a list like table 7-3. Note that checkpoints have been sequenced as much as possible so the less expensive tests get done early and the more expensive commitments are postponed until later on.

Limiting the Downside

Table 7-3 includes the cost of reaching each checkpoint. This is one of the most valuable aspects of a discovery-driven plan. Because you've thought about how much it will cost to achieve that checkpoint, you know exactly at any point in time what your downside exposure is. If you reach the checkpoint and your assumptions are not validated, you have no obligation to continue down the same path. You can stop, re-think, redirect, or change what you're doing, but you have absolutely contained your exposure.

Ron Pierantozzi, our colleague from Air Products, found this a powerful argument to use when he was attempting to gain budget approval for projects that were so uncertain that a realistic net present value (NPV) calculation is not possible. In conversations with his CFO, he laid out the checkpoint he would like to reach, assuring the CFO that

TABLE 7-3

Working checkpoint/assumption list

Checkpoint number	Checkpoint event	Assumptions tested	Cost
1	Market study	1, 2 3, 5, etc.	$3K
2	Industry analysis	8, 9, etc.	$10K
3	Feasibility study	Etc.	$25K
3	Product samples		$6K
4	Focus groups studies		$14K
5	Advertising study		$25K
6	Human resource and manpower study		$25K
7	Market research: conjoint analyses		$25K
8	Trials with beta users		$50K
9	Focus group discussions with beta users		$25K
10	Pilot plant		$100K
11	Pilot marketing campaign		$80K
12	Plant design and site acquisition		$4M
13	Pilot sales recruitment and training		$75K
14	Plant construction launch line 1		$3M
15	Manufacturing recruitment and training		$200K
16	Plant commissioning		$150K
17	Sales recruitment and training		$250K
18	Product launch		$750K
19	Full-scale plant construction launch		$1.5M

the company would not be exposed to any more risk than the cost to achieve that checkpoint. This allowed the financial side of the house to feel far more comfortable with taking risks than if Pierantozzi had tried to get funding for the whole project. It also created alignment between the new-business-development group and the finance group because both parties were working with common expectations for what was going to happen next. What's more, the evaluations were being done in a way that was attuned to the unfolding of the evolving business, not on an artificial calendar review schedule.

Team Checkpoint-Review Meetings

The checkpoint-review meeting is where the disciplines of DDP come together. Prior to the meeting, everyone responsible for a significant assumption needs to go back and update the latest information. These inputs should be collated and the DDP documents updated. At the checkpoint-review meeting, the goal is to get a clear sense of what has been learned, what is still missing, and how the team will get to the next step.

It is key that people with responsibility for significant assumptions are involved and engaged in the meeting. The tone is also important—the goal is not to prove that you were right or wrong in making an assumption. The goal is to get to the best information you can. So the dialogue needs to be very candid, without any of the gotchas that characterize many conventional project-review meetings. Finding you are wrong about an assumption is actually a good thing if you've identified it and caught it, hopefully, early. We encourage you always to think with enormous parsimony, which entails finding imaginative ways to minimize investments and postpone large-cost commitments until critical assumptions have been tested.

Among the activities that you may wish to include explicitly in your project review is to have participants reestimate the ranges of their assumptions. As we suggested in chapter 6, these ranges should narrow as the team learns. Our preference is to go through the assumptions one at a time and ask the team members to challenge any number they feel uncomfortable with, provide an alternative number, and offer their rationale for the number they propose. This allows reasonable debate among team members, who can then agree on the rationale for setting the highest, the lowest, and the most likely values for each variable.

It is critical to move fairly quickly through this process. Don't get bogged down in details, since at this stage it is not clear which numbers are really going to matter. The objective is to fairly quickly build a reasonable revised model of the business—a model that you all agree on, letting the ranges for the variables reflect your uncertainty or disagreement. Once the model is built, sensitivity analysis will help pinpoint the variables on which you can least afford to be wrong.

We like to structure checkpoint-review meetings almost as mini postmortems, with the idea being to foster continuous improvement. You can use the following agenda to guide the discussion:

1. What did we hope to achieve at the checkpoint?

2. What actually happened?

3. Why did it happen?

4. What have we learned—specifically, what assumptions need to be updated in our plan?

5. What does this imply for the plan as a whole?

   - How are we doing on our BareBones NPV—still positive (see chapter 4)?

   - Should the focus of the project be shifted?

   - Should we move on to the next step? If this does not seem attractive, should we change the target market? Should we consider spinning this venture out? Are there business divisions that might better be able to launch it?

   - If we feel the project needs to be shut down, what can we salvage from it (see chapter 8)?

   - Are important new assumptions or checkpoints necessary?

6. Plan to move to the next step if the business seems viable.

Sometimes it pays to design a relatively expensive test just to ensure that you do not regret being wrong on a much more expensive investment later. When Japan's Kao Corporation (known in Japan as a soap and cosmetics manufacturer) went into the manufacture of floppy disks as a result of its deep knowledge of surfactant technology, Kao felt it was important to determine user acceptance of a disk with the Kao name on it. So the firm subcontracted with a conventional manufacturer of floppy disks for a private-label version, to which Kao attached its own name. The technical buyers to whom Kao sent the disks approved the quality and listed Kao as an approved supplier, thus proving that the Kao name would not be an obstacle to adoption.

We have some important observations about the range-setting process. Those who put together the original plan have no need to be defensive—the plan is not right, anyway—and what matters is how to get it as right as possible by eliciting the judgment and opinions of the expert people in the room. In our experience, the process is particularly valuable for eliciting expertise. If a participant is concerned about a number, his or her obligation is to say why and to suggest an alternative number. In this way, the expertise that is present can be drawn out nonconfrontationally and focused where it is best suited.

If I have no knowledge with respect to a number, I should feel comfortable to remain silent and let others discuss it. (If you have nothing to say, don't waste time saying it!) But if someone says nothing about an assumption, then it means that de facto, the person can live with it. But it also means that the silent participants concur with the plan as is. They have abdicated the right to say later that they thought the number was wrong.

At this meeting, it is crucial that the participants weigh in with the best information that they have. What we don't want is someone eight weeks later saying "Oh, I knew that." That is definitely not in keeping with the spirit of a discovery-driven plan. So if you are part of a checkpoint-review meeting, your obligation is to be as thoughtful and frank as you can.

By the time we have finished this process, it is *our* plan, not *my* plan. It is the best we can do. Not right, not certain, but the best we can do.

If you are running the meeting, bear in mind these points:

- Try to elicit relevant feedback from everyone.

- Try to stay focused on the agenda—in particular, the team should not assume that the project is moving to the next step without explicitly asking that question.

- Keep the meeting as short as possible—you don't want people ducking out of checkpoint reviews because the meetings go on forever.

- Don't get obsessive about details, particularly in the early-stage ventures. You can get totally bogged down trying futilely to make detailed plans for fundamentally uncertain things.

In chapter 5, we introduced Tom Schuler and the DuPont buildings innovations team, which succeeded in driving 20 percent growth compounded every year in a sector that many would describe as struggling. Checkpoint meetings, project redirection, and stopping have become part of the fabric of the way the group operates. Indeed, Schuler's management practices reflect many of the essential disciplines of discovery-driven growth: making a distinction between core, low-uncertainty investments and options; killing projects early before they are too expensive; and being unafraid to redirect the business. He explains some of the distinctions between conventional and discovery-driven approaches:

> Are core businesses and the new businesses the same? God no. That's probably the biggest thing we are doing now, making that distinction. We rely on six sigma a lot to quantify the product we are going after if it's in the core. If you look at six sigma from a marketer's standpoint, you get the voice of the customer, you come up with a solution, try it, tweak it, spread it like wildfire. That's good marketing in the core business. As we go into markets where we're trying to learn, what we've gotten better at is trying small things. If they are successful, we spread them like wildfire. If not, we kill them quickly. The approach has allowed us to learn a lot of stuff about markets that we didn't know before.[5]

Quantifying Your Insight About When to Stop

In chapter 4, we introduced the BareBones NPV concept, which takes the plan numbers and calculates a rough-and-ready NPV based on your assessment of the "profit wave" of the business: how long the launch will take, how long you will be able to run your profits before competitive attack, and how fast competition will erode your profits.

We can use these numbers to calculate an *allowable investment to next checkpoint*, which specifies the maximum you should be willing to spend to get from where you are to the next checkpoint event. Here is a walk-through:

> You start by defining an *appetite factor*. This is your appetite for risking the loss you will incur if your project fails at the next checkpoint. The concept is similar to a "stop-loss" instruction for an investor, meaning that your broker would sell a security once it dips below a certain threshold. The appetite factor ideally is a number that the whole project team can endorse.
>
> Next, calculate a revised BareBones NPV using your updated assumptions after the checkpoint-review meeting. This gives you what you currently expect the performance of the venture to be. Using the software, in the BioBarrier case, this BareBones NPV came to $11 million.
>
> Next, enter into your deliverables specification spreadsheet the worst values of the ranges of your most recent assumptions. In other words, if things go really wrong, how bad could things get?
>
> Using the BareBones NPV calculator, enter the worst-case assumptions to calculate a worst-case NPV. In the BioBarrier case, this came to negative $63 million.
>
> Now calculate the difference between the worst-case and current expected BareBones NPV. We call this the *downside spread*. In the BioBarrier case, the downside spread came to $74 million ($11 million − [−$63 million]).

The next step is to honor the options principal of containing downside risk in order to pursue upside opportunity. To do this, divide your BareBones NPV by the downside spread to get a *spread ratio*. In the BioBarrier case, the ratio is 0.15 ($11 million ÷ $74 million).

Finally, multiply your revised BareBones NPV by the spread ratio. This gives you the maximum investment you should consider making to get to the next checkpoint—in other words, the most you should risk to go to the next checkpoint. In the BioBarrier case, this came to $1.65 million ($11 million × 0.15). In other words, your maximum investment to get to the next checkpoint is $1.65 million.

This is where the appetite factor comes in. You can hedge your downside even further by applying your appetite factor, which is your choice of the percentage of the maximum investment to get to the next checkpoint. In the BioBarrier case, the managers selected an appetite factor of 10 percent of the maximum investment. This gave an allowable investment of $167,000 (10 percent of $1.65 million). In other words, if going to the next checkpoint is going to cost more than $165,000, the project is a candidate for discontinuation.

Progress to Subsequent Checkpoints

Now let's see what happens as the project progresses and the ranges of assumptions begin to shift. Returning to the BioBarrier example, let's say that after going through the first few checkpoints and doing market analyses, some focus-group work, and field testing, you have reduced the ranges of your discovery-driven plan to the point that the revised BareBones NPV is $12 million and the new worst-case NPV is negative $3 million.

The downside spread would now be $15 million ($12 million – [–$3 million]).

The spread ratio would now be 0.80 ($12 million ÷ $15 million).

The maximum investment would be $9.6 million (0.80 × $12 million).

And applying the appetite factor of 10 percent would yield an allowable investment of $960,000 (10 percent of $9.6 million) to get to the next checkpoint.

Remember, your goal is to maximize the upside of your investment while limiting the downside. By using this allowable figure, we are ensuring that the worse your potential downside (worst-case NPV), the less you are allowed to spend to move forward, because the increased spread drags down your spread ratio. On the other hand, the greater the expected upside, the more the higher revised BareBones NPV increases your spread ratio and the more leeway your project gets.

The allowable-investment rule forces you to come up with low-cost checkpoints to test assumptions early on, yet also allows you to spend imagination instead of money to pursue high-potential projects. This decision criterion also ensures that you continue to pursue only the best opportunities.

We repeat that you should avoid getting obsessed with false precision. BareBones NPV calculations are perfectly adequate, especially early on in the project. Nor should you fret about letting a "big one get away"—there will be other potential blockbuster opportunities.[6]

At each checkpoint, we apply three decision rules:

Does the revised BareBones NPV continue to *promise more than do alternative projects* that are competing for resources and talent? If the NPV remains higher than competing projects, the project should be continued according to the revised discovery-driven plan. If not, it should be considered for disengagement or be put on hold, and the resources should be committed to a project with more promise.

If the revised BareBones NPV is the *same as or better than it was at the previous checkpoint* and better than that of alternative projects, the project should obviously go forward. Nevertheless, the team still needs to look at whether redirection could enhance the emergent opportunity (perhaps by accelerating the project or entering into a joint venture or alliance to speed up technology development or market access).

If the revised BareBones NPV numbers are *less than* at the previous checkpoint, is the estimated investment to get to the next checkpoint less than the allowable investment? If not, either consider disengagement or create a lower-cost route to the next checkpoint.

If your cost to the next checkpoint exceeds the allowable investment, the onus is on the team to justify not exiting the project.

Using More Sophisticated Analyses

As additional input to your checkpoint-review meetings, you might also wish to incorporate some of the more sophisticated analyses we talked about in chapter 6. These can often give you additional insights. For instance, as your venture moves forward, the ranges of outcomes in your plan should contract. In other words, you should be able to make predictions with more confidence. If this is not happening, you are not learning, which is the objective of DDP, so you need to ask why the project should not be redirected or discontinued.

Similarly, the impact of the most important variables in your staircase chart should shrink as you redirect your plan in such a way that the assumptions with the greatest effect on the bottom line are tested.

Creating the Checkpoint/Assumption Table

The following steps will lead you through this process.

1. Develop your list of key checkpoints (no more than twenty at the outset, please) that you think will be key development

points in the progress of your venture. Lay them out in the top of a checkpoint/assumption list (as in table 7-2).

2. Dig out your list of key assumptions. For each assumption, note at which checkpoint new information is likely to be discovered. There may be multiple checkpoints relevant to a given assumption. Place a check mark wherever that assumption should be reviewed at a checkpoint.

   For important assumptions, you should have multiple checkpoints, perhaps rough at first, that narrow the range as you move through the plan. You may even have to design a checkpoint to test the most sensitive assumptions, including disqualifier checkpoints for these critical assumptions.

3. Scrutinize the table—are there any empty rows? These are assumptions with no checkpoint. Create or add a checkpoint. Any empty columns? These are checkpoints with no assumptions tested—which is a wasted opportunity to learn.

4. Estimate the cost of achieving the checkpoints. Are there any that will inexpensively test major assumptions? Try to move those checkpoints to as early in the process as possible. Will any checkpoints be risky, irreversible, or expensive? Try to move those as far back in the process as possible.

5. Working with your team, determine how the plan will get to the next checkpoint and what it will cost. If this is more than the threshold investment to the next checkpoint, you need to find a way of doing it for less—you may need to involve your management structure here if resources are required.

6. After the checkpoint, hold a checkpoint-review meeting with your team. Depending on the outcome, you may need to loop back with your venture board to keep it updated on key developments.

7. Revise your discovery-driven plan, and develop the plan to get to the next checkpoint.

Now, we'll show how to incorporate these tools with an example from the BioBarrier venture.

Specific Example of Checkpoint/Assumption Table: BioBarrier

The result of your analyses and discussions should be a completed checkpoint/assumption table for thinking through when you are going to test which assumptions (and in what order—trying to push back the most expensive or inflexible assumption tests). For the BioBarrier project, the combination of checkpoints and assumptions looked like the one in table 7-3, which we've fleshed out in table 7-4.

After Each Review Meeting . . .

Don't waste all that creative thinking that took place during the review meeting. Now is the time for someone to revise the plan documents, capture the main conclusions, and make sure everyone is clear on what needs to happen at the next step, including who will be responsible for which assumptions, while the group builds toward the next checkpoint. If you are continuing with the venture, get started with the learning you'll need to do before you can get to the next checkpoint.

Let's say the worst happens and that during the review, you come to the unavoidable conclusion that it doesn't make sense for the initiative to go forward and that you will have to shut it down. The next chapter discusses this possibility and how you can handle the important step of disengagement.

ACTION STEPS

1. Working with your team, develop your list of the most significant checkpoints that the venture will go through. Estimate the cost of achieving each checkpoint.

TABLE 7-4

BioBarrier checkpoint/assumption list

Checkpoint number	Checkpoint event	Assumptions tested	Cost
1	Market study	All	$3K
2	Industry analysis	All	$10K
3	Feasibility study	All	$25K
3	Product samples	1, 3, 4, 5	$6K
4	Focus groups studies	1, 3, 4	$14K
5	Advertising study	2	$25K
6	Human resource and manpower study	7, 8, 12, 13, 14	$25K
7	Market research: conjoint analyses	1, 3	$25K
8	Trials with beta users	1, 2, 3, 4, 5	$50K
9	Focus group discussions with beta users	1, 3, 4	$25K
10	Pilot plant	9, 10, 11, 15, 16, 17	$100K
11	Pilot marketing campaign	1, 3, 4, 6, 7, 8, 17	$80K
12	Plant design and site acquisition	18, 20	$2M
13	Pilot sales recruitment and training	1, 4, 5, 6	$75K
14	Plant construction launch line 1	9, 10, 11, 20	$2.75M
15	Manufacturing recruitment and training	12, 13, 14, 15, 16, 17	$100K
16	Plant commissioning	9, 11, 12, 15, 16,17, 18, 20	$150K
17	Sales recruitment and training	1, 3, 4, 5, 6, 7, 8	$250K
18	Product launch	All	$750K
19	Full-scale plant construction launch	All	$4M

2. Create the checkpoint/assumption list by flagging which assumptions will be tested at which checkpoint.

3. Add ranges to your assumptions.

4. Calculate a BareBones NPV and a worst-case NPV.

5. If you wish, you can use the staircase software to model the sensitivity of the whole plan to variations in certain assumptions. This will influence your decisions about creating or sequencing early checkpoints.

6. Working with your team, decide in what sequence you will prioritize the checkpoints. Put the most expensive ones and those that will cause significant losses of flexibility later; put in early the less expensive ones or those that reduce your uncertainty the most. Make sure that the person responsible for each key assumption is aware of his or her responsibility to document it and watch what is happening.

7. When you reach a checkpoint, calculate the threshold investment and convene a checkpoint-review meeting. (Prior to the meeting, get updated checkpoints and rerun the plan.) At the meeting, discuss what you have learned and determine the next steps, using the formats we've described above.

8. If you decide your project can go forward either in its current incarnation or in a redirected state, continue with assumption testing and checkpoint reviews.

9. If you conclude that your project should not go forward, pay extra attention to the next chapter, which discusses disengagement.

CHAPTER EIGHT

Practicing the Necessary Art
of Disengagement

For all the effort that you may have put into developing each of the discovery-driven plans for your growth portfolio, it's important to remember that even with great planning and strict discipline, many of your projects, particularly the bold ones, are unlikely to achieve commercial success. In pursuing a portfolio of growth initiatives, you will find that, sadly, the bulk of them will never emerge as major growth drivers.[1] Indeed, one study argues that it takes three thousand raw ideas to result in one commercial success.[2]

Lack of success does not need to be a terrible result.[3] Provided that you keep your disappointments cheap, you can afford a lot of them. As we pointed out in chapter 7, you need to consider whether redirecting the project—by spinning it off, spinning it "in," or salvaging some aspect of it—is an option.[4]

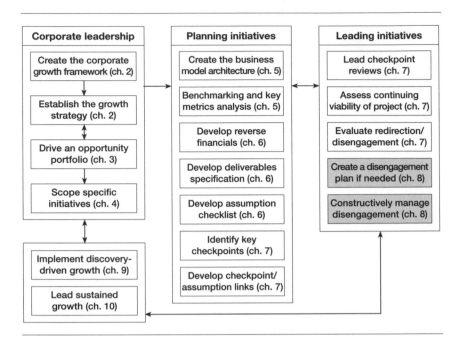

Corporate leadership	Planning initiatives	Leading initiatives
Create the corporate growth framework (ch. 2)	Create the business model architecture (ch. 5)	Lead checkpoint reviews (ch. 7)
Establish the growth strategy (ch. 2)	Benchmarking and key metrics analysis (ch. 5)	Assess continuing viability of project (ch. 7)
Drive an opportunity portfolio (ch. 3)	Develop reverse financials (ch. 6)	Evaluate redirection/ disengagement (ch. 7)
Scope specific initiatives (ch. 4)	Develop deliverables specification (ch. 6)	Create a disengagement plan if needed (ch. 8)
	Develop assumption checklist (ch. 6)	Constructively manage disengagement (ch. 8)
Implement discovery-driven growth (ch. 9)	Identify key checkpoints (ch. 7)	
Lead sustained growth (ch. 10)	Develop checkpoint/ assumption links (ch. 7)	

But even these redirecting efforts may not work, and you may conclude that rather than let the project continue to sap organizational resources, you need to bite the bullet and shut it down. We call this process *pruning.* Just as a fruit tree yields more if the mass of its old, low-yield, and resource-sapping branches are pruned, so a business intent on growth needs to prune projects that are not promising yet are still consuming resources. The goal is to free up resources that are being been directed to unproductive activities and dead ends and shift them to higher-priority, more attractive opportunities. Pruning is one of the toughest, but one of the most important tasks you can undertake when you pursue innovative growth. There is a temptation to keep going on—a temptation that escalates as the time, energy, and resources invested in the project increase.[5] The tragedy is that the energy of good people and the effectiveness of your organization can be compromised by being entrapped in what venture capitalists call "living dead" projects.

Not every initiative will require disengagement. But when it does, you can refer to the shaded areas on the road map to gain an understanding of where disengagement fits into discovery-driven growth.

Systematic Steps to Disengagement

Disengagement, which is essentially the ramping-down of a discovery-driven initiative, should also be tackled with a systematic approach.

Step 1: Assess what is keeping the team engaged with the initiative. You need to understand whether the team members' commitment to continue is realistic or whether their persistence stems from perfectly natural but impractical emotional reasons. If it's emotional, come up with a plan to help them separate their feelings of commitment from the decision to terminate and address the personal and organizational downsides that result from disengaging.

Remember the plan was uncertain to begin with, so there can be no question of failure—how can you fail if you had no idea of the outcome to start with? Therefore, instead of failure or even disappointment, we prefer to talk about disengagement, just like a smart military leader who disengages from a skirmish rather than getting sucked into a rout.

Step 2: Develop a disengagement plan, which will include ways to address the negative fallout of disengagement both in stakeholder and in interpersonal terms, but also analyzes what has been learned and what opportunities have been created. Sometimes, there can be enormous value in recouping aspects of the growth initiative and diverting them to profitable uses elsewhere.

Step 3: Systematically assign responsibilities for managing damage control and identifying disengagement opportunities.

Escalation of Commitment to a Project

Escalation of commitment refers to situations in which, despite all the evidence of impending disaster, people and organizations keep adding resources to a project that is going monumentally off the rails. Barry Staw and his colleagues have done exceptional work studying the phenomenon, which has occurred with large public-sector projects (Expo '86) and significant private projects (the Shoreham Nuclear Power Plant).[6] Escalation is often based on the best of intentions. The researchers have identified three major sources of entrapment in a failed initiative: psychological entrapment, in which team members feel personally committed to stay the course; rationalized entrapment, in which team members feel that success is just around the corner; and social entrapment, which makes team members reluctant to withdraw from a project because of commitments they have made to each other and to outside parties.

If your project fails or comes close to failing the threshold test that we proposed in chapter 7, it is important to consider the possibility that your team is victim to the subtle development of entrapment. A simple way to do this is with a pen-and-pencil test (see table 8-1) that you can ask each team member to submit anonymously (of course, you could also put it on the Web, and collate the answers that way). Ask each person to check off the "yes" or "no" columns in response to each question. A simple test for escalation? If you have a third or more "yes" answers, your team is at risk of escalated commitment.

Each of these questions reflects a reason why in the past some pretty smart, successful people have consciously or unconsciously continued committing their talent and resources to projects that reasonably should have been shut down. If your project is not faring as well as you had hoped (and remember, more often than not, this will happen), we suggest you have a frank discussion with your team members about how vulnerable your team is to these sometimes subtle pressures. If these forces are overcoming people's better judgment, you are going to have to make a tough call.

TABLE 8-1

Is your team at risk for escalation of commitment?

Does this statement reflect how most people on the team feel at the moment?	Yes	No
I feel we will lose the respect of others if this project is shut down—nobody respects a failure.		
Giving up now would just be an admission of weakness.		
Stopping this project would have a negative effect on my career: bonus, raise, promotion, or position.		
Stopping this project would have a negative effect on the rest of the team's careers: bonus, raise, promotion, or position.		
We made a public commitment to this project.		
It will destroy our record of past success.		
We have had some good results—it would be premature to stop the project now.		
There will be a big payoff if we succeed in the end.		
We're nearly at a turning point; it would be a shame to stop now, when we are so close.		
We have already spent a lot of time and money, which would be wasted if we stopped now.		
It would cost us more to stop now than it would to finish the project.		
We won't get anything back if we close the project now.		
Our part of the business is counting on us to succeed.		
People who want us to fail (rivals, enemies, competitors) will gloat.		
A lot of people are depending on us to succeed here.		
A lot of people left steady, secure positions to join this project.		
We've made commitments to outside parties that depend on the success of the project: investors, suppliers, distributors, customers.		
We've made commitments to inside parties to continue with the project: the board, top management, other divisions, employees.		
The firm's reputation with banks and investment analysts has been staked on the success of this project.		
The firm's reputation with regional, national or foreign government officials has been staked on the success of this project.		

If you do decide to shut down the project, the issues presented in table 8-1 are the ones that are likely to form the biggest part of the heartache. If you are savvy, you'll figure out a way to make the pain of each very legitimate issue easier to bear. For instance, let's say the technical people will be devastated at the loss of reputation that shutting the project down might cause. Can you identify and publicize some significant technological accomplishments as a demonstration of excellent performance, even if the project in which these accomplishments were developed didn't work out? The plan for handling such issues should be part of your overall disengagement plan.

Disengagement Planning

When innovative efforts produce inadequate results and are viewed strictly as failures, a great deal of potential value is lost. People overlook the advantages of what was learned during the growth initiative—things like newly created knowledge, technologies and assets, or increases in people's skills and other know-how.[7] If you elect to discontinue a project, you need to develop a disengagement plan. It's just as important as the business plan you may have used to set up your growth initiative, but perhaps because people are so averse to a failure, it is often neglected, leaving value on the table and a lot more misery than is necessary.

The disengagement plan should be a short (maximum five-page) but well-crafted, deeply considered document developed by the venture team in conjunction with senior managers. It formally addresses setting up damage control of any negative fallout from disengagement and extracting the maximum learning and opportunity from the project.

Failure to do this has repeatedly occasioned huge opportunity losses to firms that could have gleaned major gains from what was learned. In one bank project we analyzed, management shut down a project when problems elsewhere in the company made it difficult to continue funding the development of the new business. In essence, the project managers then "turned off the lights and shut the door." Senior management never realized, nor did anyone tell the managers, that the project had left behind a revolutionary technology for transmitting vast amounts of data using signal compression, a technology at least seven years ahead of its time. The Internet came into commercial use six years later, and today, fast data processing is key to the business model of many rapidly growing firms. Huge profits could have been reaped by licensing the technology, if only someone in the bank had thought about recouping.

Damage Control

The first challenge with disengagement is damage control. Table 8-2 provides a structured way of thinking through how you can contain the damage that might be caused by shutting down the project. In the first column, list all the stakeholders who will be disappointed by the disengagement. In the second column, specify what the disappointed party is hoping for, but will not receive. A note here: your team may erroneously assume that the stakeholders have certain disappointments—so be sure to check these disappointed expectations before you expend effort fixing what is not broken! In the third column, list the steps that could be taken to bridge the disappointment. These might range from simply conveying to the stakeholders that their expectations will not be met, with apologies, to making formal restitution. The fourth column specifies who is responsible for ensuring that this particular stakeholder has come to terms with the disappointing outcome. The final column, "Closure," represents the event that will be taken as evidence that the disappointed party has accepted the conclusion. This last column is important because people will tend to avoid the unpleasant task of damage control and need to know that the damage has not been controlled until the involved parties have reached closure, however tough this may be for the messenger.

TABLE 8-2

Damage-control plan for disappointed stakeholders

Stakeholder	Expectations of stakeholder	Action steps to redress disappointment	Who in team will redress?	Closure

Exploitation of Positives

The second challenge with disengagement is to extract the positive from the experience. The positive side of the disengagement plan comprises two parts. First is the after-action review, in which your team will try to extract the maximum amount of learning from its experiences with the project.[8] Your discovery-driven plan will have yielded many places where the conversion of assumptions to knowledge led to significant learning and valuable new insights. Think of this exercise as a way of crystallizing and documenting them. You take each major topic (we've listed some candidate topics in table 8-3), document your original assumptions and what information they were based on, what you have learned since, and what the new insights are.

This project-insight chart provides the backdrop for the last and most important document, the disengagement opportunity review, which specifies the opportunities that the disengagement might create (table 8-4). In such a review, the team can unleash its creativity in finding applications for what has been learned. What we are after is an assessment of what opportunities might still be available even though the team has decided to disengage. Here, much can be done to recoup the effort and expense that went into the project and to recoup morale that may have been eroded in the project's battle for progress. If your team members can end the project recognizing that it was the project,

TABLE 8-3

Project insights

Learning topic	Original assumption and basis	Key learning and reason	New insights
Product			
Customers			
Channels			
Technology			
People			
Processes			
Stakeholders			

and not them, that did not succeed, you will have considerably rebuilt any lost morale and confidence.[9] You could also gain serious economic benefits from this analysis: M. A. Maidique and B. J. Zirger's 1985 longitudinal study of a sample of major new product innovation successes traced the source of these triumphs to what the firm had learned from earlier abject failures.[10] Among the triumphs was the evolution of the Thunderbird and the Mustang from what Ford had learned from the Edsel fiasco, and the development of the IBM System 360 from what IBM had learned from its Stretch computer debacle.

In table 8-4, the first column lists many of the ways in which the new insights derived from the project might be deployed. The team should be challenged to fill in as many as it can. The second column identifies the specific candidates for the application. The third column specifies the insight or outcome that can be exploited; this information is often drawn from table 8-3. The final column identifies the key person who has signed up for responsibility to promulgate the opportunity.

Let's see how this worked in the case of an actual disengagement.

TABLE 8-4

Disengagement opportunity review

	Candidate	Insight or result	Key person
Opportunities for knowledge transfer			
To other divisions			
To other products			
To other markets			
To improve operating processes			
To improve management processes			
To customers			
To distributors			
To suppliers			
To partners			
Economic opportunities			
Spin-in			
Spin-off			
Licensing			
Sale of knowledge			
Joint venture			
Other			

From Initial Framing to Disengagement: The Evolution of the SmartFilm Project

A real-life example illustrates the disengagement of a growth initiative. Called the SmartFilm project, the initiative was intended to take the parent company, Chemco, into an entirely new materials area.

The case has been disguised in a way that allows you to get the gist of how to disengage, yet at the same time protects the confidentiality of the company and the people involved. Therefore, much of the technical and market data is deliberately imprecise.

SmartFilm, a film for coating transparent or reflective surfaces, allowed the user to vary the reflectivity of those surfaces. Major potential markets were buildings, factories, automobiles and other transportation vehicles, and all types of signage, ranging from billboards to wall displays.

There was considerable uncertainty among the Chemco staff about the market size, growth rate, and price required for the long-term viable commercial success of SmartFilm. There was also considerable technical uncertainty about how to achieve the quality and performance criteria of the coated film, which varied by application. The firm needed to better understand potential competition for other new emerging technologies that might meet the same needs that the Smart-Film product met.

A main differentiator for SmartFilm was that changing surface reflectivity of the film allowed the user to modify, through electromagnetic switching, the light emanating or being reflected from the surface. The technology represented an entrée into a new type of market for Chemco, which extended its reach into performance materials. All competing applications required physical changes, which were slow, cumbersome, and expensive.

Chemco appeared to be the first to market in this space, as competing licensees had not yet produced a commercially viable product. Even better, several customers were ready to place orders immediately for small quantities of the film, provided that the SmartFilm product could meet their minimum performance criteria. The major project risks were high uncertainty about market growth and overall size and whether the film could be produced at low enough cost. There was also lack of clarity as to which coating process would be used. To meet the initial potential customers' expectations, the team would have to figure out how to significantly increase quality and performance standards, while simultaneously meeting cost targets.

Project Preliminaries

The SmartFilm project got going in 2004 and was originally sponsored by the Corporate Development Office (CDO), the primary new-ventures unit within Chemco. The chief technology officer (CTO), in conjunction with the marketing division of Chemco's Emulsion Division, had licensed the technology from an external source.

Once preliminary technical and marketing work was completed and the license was secured, the SmartFilm project was transferred to one of the core business groups, the Chemicals Division group, under the guidance of Kara Camille, the SmartFilm project director. Camille reported to a steering committee (composed of the division manager for chemicals, the CTO, and the chief marketing officer), which met quarterly to review all the projects in the Chemco portfolio.

The role of the steering committee was mainly for ratification. At each quarterly meeting, members of the committee asked penetrating questions about progress on the plan. They provided advice where they felt competent and ratified the requests for resources to move to the next checkpoint.

Framing the Project

Camille was very aware that as a big player in its industry, Chemco needed high-volume markets and at least $5 million in profits. Although niche customers might be willing to pay a high price for the coated film initially, Camille believed that to achieve scale in a mass market sufficient to meet Chemco's growth challenges, prices would have to fall dramatically, to as low as $10 per pound of film. The initial frame she assembled with her team appears in table 8-5.

As you can see, the volume challenges for the project were considerable. If Chemco needed to generate $5 million in profits from material that would sell for as little as $10 per pound, applied as film one-thousandth of an inch thick, Camille would have to sell film for 300 million square feet of various surfaces. Every year.

Assuming that SmartFilm achieves a maximum of 10 percent of the market for surfaces needing reflection control, this implied a minimum total market of 3 billion square feet. Clearly, this would have to

TABLE 8-5

Initial frame for SmartFilm project

Hypothetical specification

Required profits	$5 million
Required margin	20%
Required revenues	$25 million
Unit of business for product	Pounds
Expected price per pound	$10
Required pounds	2.5 million
Unit of business for application	Square foot
Film thickness (inches)	0.001
Density of film (pounds per cubic foot)	100
Square feet required	300 million
Maximum market share	10%
Minimum total market required (square feet)	3 billion

end up as a global business, but Camille's initial assessment was that if the company could drive down the production cost and achieve the market penetration, then the project would end up with a BareBones net present value (NPV) of about $7.5 million. She decided to go forward by first testing assumptions regarding film production, quality, and cost.

At a meeting held in September 2004, Camille's steering committee authorized her to go forward with the program. In keeping with the discipline of checkpoints, Camille was authorized to spend only as many resources as were necessary to get to the first checkpoint. The committee agreed with Camille that this checkpoint would occur when a sample of SmartFilm had been tested by initial target customers in prototype mode.

Course of the Project

From October 1, 2004, until April 1, 2005, the technical team developed an improved coating that did improve film quality. The technicians worked with their marketing departments to beta-test the new material with key users. The team assumed that SmartFilm coated film now had the improved performance characteristics that the team believed would meet customer needs. But once presented with an actual sample, customer feedback dashed that assumption. While the availability of a prototype massively improved the dialogue, the message was not good for SmartFilm. Customers realized that what they really needed was an even higher minimum performance level in reliability, a level that so far Camille's team had been unable to meet. Camille concluded that until the project could deliver to that level, she could not reliably generate sales of the product. Since she was mandated to improve on Chemco's overall margins, or at minimum match them with the new business, she didn't have the option of cutting price to create volume demand.

The challenge was then mainly a technical one: figuring out how to meet the requirements and match the price the customers wanted. The technical people appealed for more budget, staff, and time to produce the lower-cost coating needed. Camille and the technical and marketing teams developed a reverse income statement in a revised discovery-driven plan that integrated the complex and numerous assumptions the technical team had been making regarding the multiple components of the film, its manufacture, and the coating of the surfaces. By completing this discovery-driven exercise as a team, the group reached a deep understanding of the ability, limitations, and additional development that would be required to meet customer expectations.

With the latest product-cost figures included in the discovery-driven plan and the BareBones NPV, Camille decided that it would still be worth spending funds up to the threshold investment on technical development and marketing. A second checkpoint meeting was set for July 2005. This checkpoint would be a technical one. The question would be this: could the company reduce the cost of production to the level demanded by customers while it maintained product quality and reliability?

Second Checkpoint Meeting: Disengagement Decision

The second meeting was held on July 1, 2005. Based on new learning to validate and update the assumptions made before the checkpoint, the revised plan showed reductions in some important areas: the growth in demand, the duration of demand growth, applications of product, potential submarkets for offering, and time to reach critical mass of sales. The changed assumptions, with increasing costs and uncertain market growth for the future, led to a much-reduced BareBones NPV, with a threshold investment so low as to preclude any further meaningful technical development.

The team learned that it could not achieve the cost reductions needed to meet the price requirements of the market for the high-volume applications. Nor could it achieve one key performance criterion with the technology in its current form. Despite the disappointment, the decision to shut down the SmartFilm project was made by mutual agreement. Now there remained the task of constructive disengagement.

Camille first reviewed the need for damage control and developed action steps to do so. Table 8-6 depicts her damage-control plan (with the "Who will redress" column removed).

Upsides of Disengagement

At the meeting on July 1, 2005, the team at Chemco realized that they had learned from the project even though it was dropped. They had become better at understanding user needs and at defining target markets. They had developed their skills at managing development projects. They had become better at interacting with licensors and customers as the new product evolved. They had knowledge about the coatings and coated films that could be of value to other licensors. The corporate development office learned how to better evaluate projects from the start and do more frequent revisions of the assumptions used in the model. This led Camille to two sets of actions (tables 8-7 and 8-8).

TABLE 8-6

Damage-control plan for SmartFilm's disappointed stakeholders

Stakeholder	Expectations of stakeholder	Action steps to redress disappointment	Closure
Internal developers	Expectations of success, sense of personal failure	Participation in the development of discovery-driven-planning spread-sheets and assumptions	Through the exercise, reached a consensus to recommend the project be discontinued—the project failed, not them
Licensor	Expectation that the large licensing company would generate a lot of new business for them	Provided open communi-cation of all the technology and customer challenges that led to revisions in discovery-driven planning and option assessment with reasons for disengagement	Offered the licensor access to new knowledge of technology and customers that would advance any of their other licensees
Potential customers	Many customers had orders in hand, waiting for product	Engaged these customers by providing samples of the most advanced coated film for testing	Personally contacted each potential customer and explained that project could only continue con-tingent on significantly reduced expectation of ongoing price reduction, which the customers turned down

Camille's analysis provided the SmartFilm team with the backdrop for the disengagement opportunity review (table 8-8). As you can see, despite the decision to disengage, the opportunity review brought many benefits, both internal and external, to light for Chemco.

The End of the Story?

The Chemco story actually had a pretty good outcome. The new-ventures group at Chemco used its experiences to learn better tools for managing innovation, discovery-driven planning among them. These tools were applied to many other projects, four of which have now started to generate brand-new revenue for Chemco in markets that it had not previously served.

TABLE 8-7

Project insights for SmartFilm

Learning topic	Original assumption	Context	New insight
Product	Low usage of product per order is made up for by potential size of orders.	Very little coated film used on final product surface.	For profitable orders, you need huge markets—there are few of these.
Market	Large markets with few large customers are potentially profitable.	Infeasibility of the market as an appropriate market.	The tight customer margins sought by a few highly competitive customers mean your customers will want all the value.
Technology	We can license basic technology and do the market-ready technology development ourselves.	Getting market-ready technology into markets we don't know.	Better validate market readiness of technology before licensing or know the markets you are entering.
People	Good technical people in our labs can create customer-quality product.	Lab-scale production can develop high quality in sufficient quantity for big customers.	Be more willing to seek partners instead of trying to do it just in the labs.
Processes	Discovery-driven planning is a "nice to do" approach.	Entering new product and new market space at the same time.	Discovery-driven planning is essential to make the right if painful choices at the right time.

The upshot of this chapter? Just as you must get comfortable doing things that may not fit into conventional planning, you also need to become better at the disengagement process. In a well-run portfolio of initiatives, most will eventually be disengaged in some way. It doesn't have to be a miserable experience, nor must it have the negative organizational consequences we often observe.

ACTION STEPS

1. Review the key assumptions and financials of your plan at major checkpoints. Calculate your threshold for the next checkpoint. If you cannot reduce costs to the next checkpoint below the threshold, or if key assumptions necessary for success are not

TABLE 8-8

Disengagement opportunity review

	Candidate	Insight or result	Key person
Internal opportunities for knowledge transfer			
To technology licensing	Chief technology officer	Either license market-ready technology or know the markets you are entering. When go to license, understand market readiness.	SmartFilm technology manager
To business development	Business development office	For low per-usage products, for profitable orders you need huge markets or additional benefit to other offerings.	Camille
To marketing	Divisional marketing managers	The tight customer margins sought by a few highly competitive customers mean your customers will want all the profits in the value chain.	SmartFilm marketing manager
To technology development	Chief technology officer, marketing	Lab-scale production may not be able to develop samples of commercial quality to secure initial orders.	SmartFilm technology manager
To improve management processes	Strategic planning and business development office	Discovery-driven planning is essential to make the right, if painful, choices at the right time.	Camille
External opportunities			
Spin-in	Chemco project	Technical knowledge is gained in a new part of the supply chain (film) applicable to another Chemco project.	Chemco project manager
License-back	Licensor	Potential for sale of new SmartFilm knowledge.	Chemco licensing officer
Sale of knowledge	Other licensees	End-use advisory and development services.	Chemco technical department

being increasingly borne out, you may need to consider disengagement.

2. If this is the case, work your way through the escalation-of-commitment questionnaire with your team (ideally, have everyone complete the pages anonymously and have the aggregated results hand in so that you can work with live data). Make sure

people are able to separate the emotional impulses that keep them tied to the project and the logical reasons for continuing to do it.

3. If there is evidence of escalation of commitment and the financials don't seem to be working out, prepare a disengagement plan.

4. Prepare a damage-control plan, and assign people to deliver closure for each item in the plan.

5. Review your key lessons from the projects, and identify and document the key insights from this learning.

6. Identify disengagement opportunities that have emerged from the project, despite being discontinued, and prepare a disengagement opportunity review in which you target specific beneficiaries and assign a team member the task of promulgating benefits to that beneficiary.

7. Since the best medicine for a project that didn't work out is to put your energies into a more promising way, try to get onto the next DDP team!

III

Making Discovery-Driven Growth Work for You

This final part of the book specifically addresses the organizational and leadership challenges of moving from a more conventional approach to growth to a discovery-driven orientation. In chapter 9, we'll share with you many anecdotes, stories, and lessons learned from companies that have implemented some of the discovery-driven-growth practices. Chapter 10 brings the book to a close by going over the core leadership challenges of discovery-driven growth. Recall, as you go through these, that the concepts apply both at the strategic level of the organization—creating a clear framework for the business, assembling a portfolio of growth projects, specifying what contribution different projects will make, and laying out criteria for success—and at the level of individual growth initiatives, for which you create a frame, specify deliverables, document your assumptions, and design a checkpoint and assumption chart.

CHAPTER NINE

Implementing Discovery-Driven Growth

We thought it would be illuminating to share some real-world examples of why some companies decided to adopt discovery-driven growth and how they implemented it. This chapter shows you the variety of approaches several firms have taken and lays out lessons learned from their experiences. These examples may help you put together your own best approach to DDG. They should also help make your implementation effort go more smoothly and help you sustain the discovery-driven mindset.

DDG is a process that has implications for corporate-level leadership, as the shaded area of our road map suggests.

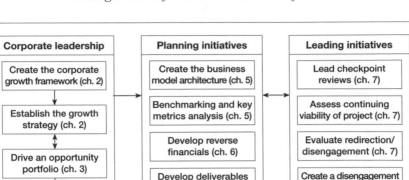

Corporate leadership	Planning initiatives	Leading initiatives
Create the corporate growth framework (ch. 2)	Create the business model architecture (ch. 5)	Lead checkpoint reviews (ch. 7)
Establish the growth strategy (ch. 2)	Benchmarking and key metrics analysis (ch. 5)	Assess continuing viability of project (ch. 7)
Drive an opportunity portfolio (ch. 3)	Develop reverse financials (ch. 6)	Evaluate redirection/ disengagement (ch. 7)
Scope specific initiatives (ch. 4)	Develop deliverables specification (ch. 6)	Create a disengagement plan if needed (ch. 8)
Implement discovery-driven growth (ch. 9)	Develop assumption checklist (ch. 6)	Constructively manage disengagement (ch. 8)
Lead sustained growth (ch. 10)	Identify key checkpoints (ch. 7)	
	Develop checkpoint/ assumption links (ch. 7)	

What Makes a Company Open to Adopting Discovery-Driven Growth?

It is axiomatic that before change can take place in an organization, there has to be some reason for it. In the case of DDG, the impetus is almost always someone who recognizes problems in the organization's current tools and approaches to growth or innovation or who is frustrated with the poor track record of growth programs. Lou Gerstner was just such a person, when he commissioned a group to find a better approach to managing growth projects at IBM.

Increasing Need for a Different Type of Growth Strategy

One way in which companies are motivated to implement DDG is when they decide to focus on growth through new business development. Nokia was one of the earliest large-scale adopters of discovery-driven planning. At the beginning of its most recent venturing push, no one knew quite how the new ventures should be planned. As the former New Ventures Organization (NVO) head explained: "We started off when NVO was set up in the summer of 1998. At that point, you said 'venture,' and people thought it equals no planning at all." Nokia encountered DDP through our writings first and then had us participate in a course that made the technique the centerpiece of its first module. The firm concluded that "putting a little bit of structure into the process was good." What attracted Nokia to the technique? The former head explained:

> It fits very well into the type of activity that we have with the ventures. They are fairly uncertain, and it's very difficult to plan ahead. Step-by-step acknowledging that we don't know everything—and don't have to know it—that is perhaps why we got into this technique. The book we had [*The Entrepreneurial Mindset*]—it was very pragmatic. Based on the book, it was quite easy to take the principles into our process.[1]

At Air Products and Chemicals, Inc., a new business development function was established in 2001 to explore new "white space" opportunities. Headed by company veteran Ron Pierantozzi, whom we've mentioned before, the group had several mandates:

- Review and develop ideas outside the current business strategies.

- Incubate new business opportunities.

- Take equity investments in new technology platforms.

As he evaluated the practices then in use for the development of innovative ideas (among them the popular stage-gate methodology for project evaluation), Pierantozzi decided that the new group required a comprehensive set of new tools.

At Swiss Reinsurance, its Leadership Academy (as it is now called) was the impetus for introducing the opportunity portfolio to the firm. Swiss Re had been battered by 9/11 and subsequent calls on its capital and was then focusing primarily on its core business. The head of the strategy office was, however, looking to support entry into new growth areas. Seeing our opportunity portfolio map, the executive decided that the tool could help organize the fledgling growth efforts. The opportunity portfolio was first presented to a pilot group at a workshop in early 2004. After an enthusiastic reception, it was presented to the CEO and eventually the executive board, who decided that this would be the tool to use for reviewing growth progress on a monthly basis.

Senior leaders with a hunger for new ideas can also provide impetus to adopt a growth strategy. Before succumbing to the destructive effects of its ill-advised acquisitive growth program, Fortis, the European financial services powerhouse, was also pushing for another approach to growth that came right from the top. Count Maurice Lippens, chairman of the board of Fortis, wanted the company to become more entrepreneurial. He believed that a venturing group could be key to creating a common group culture from the various cultures the company had inherited from years of acquisitions. Inspired by the ideas presented in Gary Hamel's "Bringing Silicon Valley Inside," Lippens sponsored the formation of a venturing group.[2] Frans de Wuffel, the former general manager of corporate HR, enumerated the many reasons for doing so:

There were numerous rationales for Fortis Venturing. First, it was clearly meant as a management retention tool. We could not afford to lose the more entrepreneurial employees within the company. In a sense, business development and management development are really two sides of the same coin! Second, we really saw it as an organizational learning tool: the objective was to improve our internal ability to make a good business case and to follow up on the development of new ventures. Third, the morale issue was important too: employees have to be proud of the company they work for. Finally, we really wanted to impact the overall culture.[3]

Over the years since the company's founding, the venture group at Fortis has incubated many initiatives, including its extremely successful yacht-financing venture.

New Senior Leadership with a Growth Mandate

A change in senior executive is often the initial spark that gets organizations interested in DDP. At 3M, when James McNerney became CEO in 2000, he massively emphasized efficiency and six sigma. When he abruptly decamped for Boeing some four and a half years later, his successor, George Buckley, worried that 3M had become a less creative, more risk-averse company. He began to press his people to take more risks, to be braver, and to grow faster. One of our contacts quoted him as saying in frustration, "There is no risk so small that 3M-ers won't avoid it!" He put resources behind the goal, initiating a $100 million fund to bankroll new opportunities.[4]

This challenge of driving more innovation was picked up by one of Buckley's new executive vice presidents, who in turn formed a small (three-person) group to learn about the idea and start to train 3M-ers in how the technique worked. They developed an innovative set of training cases and went around to various 3M businesses to get the concept off the ground. They employed what is still one of our favorite techniques for demonstrating the concept: they got participants to mock up a discovery-driven plan for 3M's entry into the space tourism business! While a little off the beaten track, this exercise helped demonstrate the DDP concept without drowning in the details of an existing initiative.

Going Through a Near-Death Experience

In contrast to the other situations in which healthy companies sought to reach even higher levels of performance, our colleagues over at IBM were coping with their company's own near-death experience. As we described in chapter 1, Lou Gerstner came to the helm of a deeply troubled IBM in 1993, and he and his executive team spent the next five or six years reorienting the core business and getting the basics right.

By 1999, the senior team at IBM was interested in moving beyond fixing the core business to reigniting growth. Around that time, they ran across a very useful book, *The Alchemy of Growth*.[5] Written by consultants at McKinsey & Company, the book has been wildly influential, in our view because it gives managers a simple, practical language for thinking about growth. The core of the book breaks the growth challenge into three horizons: H1, which are basically what we would call core enhancements; H2, which we would think of as new growth platforms; and H3, which we think of as options. Yet, even though the IBM executives now had a language for thinking about H2 and H3, few of the new growth initiatives in those spaces were getting much traction.

The IBM strategic planning staff, of which our colleague Dan McGrath (no relation) is a part, then took the unusual step of doing case studies of twenty-two H2 and H3 initiatives that had not developed well. From this analysis, beginning in 2000 they developed the emerging business opportunity (EBO) program, which tackled problems of resource attrition, lack of cross-business integration, poorly aligned incentives, and other issues. While space limitations prevent us from describing the whole EBO system, its emergence fueled the desire to find new techniques for planning and budgeting, which is when IBM began to seriously explore the discovery-driven approach.[6]

Dissatisfaction with Current Approaches

Sometimes, the impetus to adopt DDP is part of a larger change to how an organization wants to tackle projects and their approval when current approaches have been insufficient. This is very common whenever a company has grown by acquisition, processes were never harmonized, and everything is being done differently and in different places. As one of our clients reported, a main driver for the adoption of DDG tools was dissatisfaction with unwieldy, inconsistent tools of planning:

> Historically, everybody has used different frameworks or methods to assess market entry or new product, etc. There has never been a consistent framework. Every time one of these proposals is made, the pain point is brought to senior management. They have to look at and make a decision on these huge twenty- to thirty-page all-numbers business cases. They would spend days looking at it. The quality of the reviews was pretty poor. The senior managers would look at the numbers and space out or, worse, pick one number and ask, why is it this way? They never really looked at the business scope and plan overall. There was never a consistent template or framework—it was always very high level or very granular. With DDP, you get a feel for the numbers, but also the market dynamics.[7]

With another firm, the major lament was that "planning has driven out strategy." The company was proficient at producing detailed strategic plan documents and budgets, but struggled to articulate clear strategic priorities. Left unsaid were major assumptions and how the company would win, particularly in uncertain growth markets. As one interviewee observed, things were either too vague (we'll sell millions by year five) or too set in stone (the launch date will be June 1, no doubt about it). Among the benefits of adopting DDP in this context were these:

> We have been able to use the reverse P&L to have people think about, "What do you mean by this business?" Even when they say, "We have no idea," we can still get to talking about the business. What would it sell for? Would it sell for twenty cents?

Could it sell for a thousand dollars? When people say "oh no" to that, it gets them to clarify their assumptions. So it's been cool for us to have a framework that allows people to be tentative, but still captures the key points of the business. It helps us identify the load-bearing assumptions.

A Serious Desire for a Different and More Aggressive Approach to Risk

Another big motivator for companies to adopt DDP was that they were eager to change the way they looked at risk. The main goal was to get a better way to deal with shared risks. As one of our colleagues observed:

> My key learning after we implemented this was that we got buy-in from senior management with regard to our list of assumptions. There would be more understanding if we didn't meet our charter. For me, it was a realization that those risks don't just belong to me as a negative asset. So it's only fair that everyone is aware of those risks and takes responsibility for them. My learning from your work is that it's my responsibility to make sure I track assumptions and update them, as well as do what I need to do to validate them when I say I'm going to . . . As you talk to higher-level people, it makes a big difference. From the bottom side, it's fabulous to know it's not your own risk. If you want brave people, they have to know that.

The main lesson we have learned is that before discovery-driven growth will be embraced by an organization, it has to be seen as part of the answer to a clearly defined and pressing need—usually for a better way to manage growth—which existing tools are not supporting effectively. Our caveat: if your firm is in the middle of a battening-down-the-hatches exercise to rescue the core, or if growth is not perceived as high on the agenda, it's difficult to create the impetus for adopting DDG.

Championing and Implementation

From the point at which someone likes the ideas behind discovery-driven strategy, a champion is important to drive adoption of the concept forward. This person may or may not be the one who originally hit on the idea, but we've found that there is almost always one person who is taking the lead to convince others in the organization that it makes sense.

Identifying a Champion

Champions for DDG vary enormously in organizational level, power, and age. At some companies, pulling an experienced and respected senior person into a new business development role to champion innovative techniques works best. This is often the case in technology-heavy companies, in which knowing who the players are and being connected to interpersonal networks is a major advantage. Similarly experienced executives might champion the idea from their existing jobs—for instance, as chief technology officer or head of R&D. At IBM, EBO leaders are usually quite experienced senior people.

In other companies, relative newcomers can find that their status as an outsider is helpful. For one thing, they are not linked to anyone's political agenda and are seen as more or less objective. We have observed, however, that newcomers to the championing task must have unwavering support from powerful people within the corporation who control resources. In the case of Swiss Re, championship of the concepts evolved. The original discovery of the idea was made by the Swiss Re academy staff. The strategy office championed the tool to the executive board and launched the analytical work. After a year or so of success with this process, a new product development group was formed to take over the opportunity portfolio work and to advocate product development across the firm more broadly. At ADP, a newcomer to the organization was hired to champion the concept and built his political network by eventually being seen as helpful to existing business leaders in meeting a mandate for growth laid down by the executive team.

It is obviously easier to implement a new way of doing things when the push comes straight from the top. At ESCO (the distribution company from chapter 2), the champion was its new CEO. Having a CEO or another "C"-suite leader as champion does tend to make it easier to get people's attention. At ADP, the CEO and CFO were the primary champions for DDP.

Often, a champion for the concept is someone who is in some way responsible for a growth mandate for the firm. This is often a line person who either is in a strategy role or has operational responsibility for a growth-oriented area (such as R&D). At 3M, as we mentioned, the CEO wanted more risk-taking, but it was an executive vice president who championed the specific tools to get that job done. Similarly, at Nokia, its president set up and strongly supported the New Ventures Organization, but the actual tools it used and the procedures it followed were chosen by the NVO leaders.

Another pattern is for the championing to be done by someone with more of a staff than a line mandate. At IBM, for instance, the EBO concept and subsequent engagement with line management was run out of the corporate strategy office and reinforced through a series of learning interventions called the *strategic learning forums*.[8] The actual EBO projects were run by senior people who were taken out of their "day jobs" in conventional businesses to focus specifically on the projects. At Swiss Re, as we mentioned, the original champions were from the executive development area.

Our work with the champions of DDG suggests that their success is a function of the extent to which they carry out the following activities:

- Develop a deep sense for how the technique will resonate in the specific context of their own organizations.

- Line up support among their peers.

- Create in the firm networks of other people who can benefit from the adoption of the idea.

- Communicate in firm-specific language the problems that discovery-driven planning can help the firm address.

It is valuable if they are able to stay in their championing role for some time. When champions change roles too soon, it's easy for the progress they have made to slip away.

Creating the Momentum for Implementation: Three Approaches

Having a champion, of course, is just the beginning. In every organization, champions next have to sell the concept to others before it can be implemented. We found that champions for discovery-driven planning used a variety of approaches, from a top-down mandate to subtle "stealth" persuasion and everything in between. In all cases, a tremendous amount of time went into persuading, training, demonstration, and face-to-face contact with key decision makers.

The top-down mandate. A firm we'll call HLE used a top-down approach to implement DDP. The concept was introduced to the firm's senior leadership in an executive seminar led by Alex van Putten, one of our colleagues. The executives subsequently hired a DDP champion (whom we'll call Sampat) from outside the firm, explicitly to ensure its implementation. Within his first month on the job, he was sent to take one of our courses. As he described it when we first met him, his mandate upon his return to HLE was to make sure the technique was embedded in the firm:

> Part of the reason I was hired was to spearhead this, to figure out how to launch it. I told them [senior management] that we had to create buzz around the company. One of the struggles has been that I did not have a live example, so when I came back

from the course, we worked out a whole DDP project that I used as an example . . . With that exemplar project, I will have that live example, so we plan to have a Web site, seminars, and "webinars," and go on a month-and-a-half road show. In short, we'll be putting it into the company in a big way. MacMillan was really helpful developing that initial example, when I couldn't figure it out.

But this was really just the marketing plan for the concept. The real teeth behind corporatewide adoption came from the mandate of senior management. As Sampat said later on:

The mandate from senior management, including the head of corporate strategy and the head of marketing, was that with any new ideas, whether they're part of the strategic plan or not—anything where they want budget from corporate—they will have to use DDP. That helped me in going to all the business units and saying that "this is going to come up, and you'll have to have a plan in place that uses this technique." Then what I did was a road show. I took the one initiative that has successfully used the technique, and we mapped it into a thirty-page deck for each session . . . We went to every business unit and did one-and-a-half-day workshops.

What senior management loves is the tangible, specific milestones . . . Now, as the business unit heads are thinking about how to succeed, they are now reaching out to me. They want me to sit down with them . . . They tried in the past, failed miserably, and now want to relaunch with the DDP concept. It's "Sampat, I need your help, let's try to figure this out."

In this case, the champion was essentially handpicked by the senior team, and the technique was sold by fiat—in effect, "Do this, or else." Although the approach was not to everyone's taste, the senior team felt that it had little time to waste in driving an organic growth agenda; the team simply couldn't allow politics and persuasion to take their timely way. To his credit, Sampat is an extraordinarily effective advocate. He took the trouble to learn and teach the process and to learn about dozens of projects going on in the company's major lines of business. He further made himself available to the company's leaders, gave all the credit for success to them, and eventually came to be seen as a valuable resource rather than an irritating roadblock to progress.

The networked venturing group. At Nokia, as we mentioned, the New Ventures Organization was essentially given the mandate to develop those systems and processes that its leaders felt would facilitate the venturing process, even if these were different from those of the established businesses. Note that unlike the top-down approach, DDG ideas were not mandated; rather, the NVO leadership was free to use them if it thought they were worthwhile. For the first couple of years, the NVO group struggled to put together the right set of tools and to link them to the right group of people. Beginning in 2000, this started to change. A partnership between the NVO head and an internal consultant was formed to drive the implementation of better planning techniques. As the head of the NVO described it:

> What we did was take one guy from the internal consulting group—he was leading it, pulling everything together. From the NVO side, there was me coordinating. It was important to have one outside person from the organization to act as a facilitator—to sit down and ask all the stupid questions Why do you do this here? Does this need to be done in this phase of the project? Could it be done later? Don't you need input from HR? Shouldn't legal be involved? We didn't take these questions as self-evident. That was quite important, to have some external person—external to the organization—creating the plan.

With the insight that improving the effectiveness of the NVO and getting the best input to their planning process would require linking the NVO ventures to the rest of the corporation, the two began to explore a new way of doing things within the NVO. Again, from the former head:

> We took a number of steps to make DDP a standard practice. The way we implemented it was first in the 2000–2001 time frame, when we started to overhaul the planning process. What we basically did is this: for us, it's about getting different functions of the organization involved. So you had to get legal, HR, and the business functions involved in the whole process and figure out how they should support the ventures. What we did was establish a working group. It took about four to six months. We basically established a project where we [would say to each support function group], "OK, these are the steps that each venture should go through. These are the ways that different support functions should support ventures in different life cycle stages," and we mapped them into one process guide.
>
> For the whole thing from start to the point where we had the process implemented, it took about four to six months. That was part of the business development activity, which was directly adapted from DDP ideas. We thought about folding in legal support—what kind of legal support [would be needed] early, what kind later, how is HR involved, how do we take into account operations and logistics, when should they be involved, what are the early-on tasks for them, how can they reduce uncertainty from their part as well?

The group effectively used DDP to create a common point of view. In the event that the ventures didn't work out, the group could recoup the learning that had been done within them, much as we suggested.[9]

The "stealth" approach. Ron Pierantozzi at Air Products and Chemicals went after implementation of DDP in an entirely different way:

> Whenever you implement new tools—there is always resistance. We had mandates about what our work processes were. What we

did instead of putting in a big program was to say that we needed to find out what tools we wanted to bring in. We piloted the tools. Our first foray into this was sending seven people to learn about DDP, marketbusters, and the other concepts at an executive program. They came back and were willing participants. We got them to pilot the new tools into a couple of projects.

We also didn't start out where there was apt to be massive resistance. We ran into resistance on real options. The whole controllership organization was resistant at first to using real options to value a technology project. So instead, we focused on looking at the technique for new geography projects, where it helped to convince management that it was a good idea to enter. There were also a number of tools we tried that didn't work for us. There were tools we piloted that we didn't use.

A key lesson for me so far is, first, to start small. Don't try to jam this into the company by making a big deal out of it. What you will find is that you will spend more time making a big deal out of it than using it . . . Starting small and finding out the value ahead of time allows you to keep it under the radar screen at the beginning.[10]

Eventually, as more people began to use the techniques to think about and implement their plans, more and more senior managers began to get comfortable with the ideas. As Pierantozzi said, eventually he successfully "co-opted" the chief technology officer to support DDP, which Pierantozzi ended up implementing across the technology organization. A big surprise was the reaction of the chief financial officer to the concept of real options. We thought that a CFO would be highly uncomfortable with the concept of real options. Well, it turned out that this executive was actually teaching a course on real options at Cornell! Somehow, his endorsement seemed to overcome the initial reluctance on the part of the controller organization.

Having successfully piloted the concepts and developed a track record of success, Pierantozzi said that he was able to more aggressively roll out the ideas:

Once we got enough people into this, we rolled it out to others. The mob rules, once a critical mass of people are using something. So that became our next activity. We created an innovation college that Air Products runs, which draws people from all across the company and planet to attend three courses a month. We developed Air Products University's innovation offerings, which consist of thirty-five courses, including a course on DDP, one on marketbusting, and one on real options. We run these in North America, Europe, and Asia for employees around the world. I still do an innovation course. We created a whole training program with the message being "We can train you to be more innovative and entrepreneurial."

We found lots of opportunity to implement the tools across a variety of businesses. People are finding creative ways to use them. One of our folks used it to understand a customer's cost structure. Developing a reverse income statement and using it to estimate what we thought they were making helped in our pricing negotiations. So we used those assumptions to set up a negotiation process to test our assumptions. We ended up with a deal with a totally different pricing model, which was much better for us.

Educating senior executives proved important to the success of the techniques as well, said Pierantozzi:

Another experience we are learning more about is how to present these ideas to senior management. One of the things you want to be careful of is putting too much emphasis on the financial piece. You know it's wrong, so why spend a lot of time on that? You really want to get them focused on the assumptions and how you go after vetting those, versus financials.

Benefits of the Three Approaches

We've illustrated three models for how the momentum to adopt DDP is harnessed: the top-down mandate, the networked venturing group, and the stealth approach. Of course, these are just illustrative of other possible approaches.

Two major lessons are worth reinforcing. First, how an organization is persuaded to adopt any new technique, discovery-driven planning included, will vary with its culture and with the current issues and challenges it is facing. Trying to impose a top-down approach on a collaborative, highly networked organization like Nokia probably wouldn't have worked very well. Trying to make a huge "program" out of DDP at Air Products and Chemicals, and thereby trapping the initiative in heavy corporate structures, would probably have undermined the novel model Pierantozzi was trying to build. And trying to build consensus in HLE, our top-down organization, when the need to change was urgent would probably have taken too long.

A second lesson is that the individuals or groups that have successfully championed DDP make it worthwhile for a broad alliance of other players, who support the program because it helps these players in some meaningful way. At HLE, it freed the senior team from hours of meaningless project reviews and helped the executives focus on strategic business issues. At Nokia, DDP helped create an infrastructure for the incubation of new business models and new technologies that subsequently proved valuable to the firm as a whole. And at Air Products and Chemicals, it helped people working on "white space," or new areas, communicate what they were doing, manage the risks, and obtain senior-level support in an intelligent way.

A Final Consideration

Implementing DDP principles is fundamentally a process of organizational change (although, hopefully, a relatively inexpensive and high-reward one). Like any organizational change, it will therefore encounter forces that are likely to delay implementation or cause resistance. We described these forces and potential ways to address them in our previous book, *MarketBusters*, so we won't go into detail here. We just encourage you to think about who is likely to oppose or resist the use of DDP and how you can overcome these resistance points before trying to implement the model.[11]

Here we have shown that the discovery-driven approach to innovation and growth has helped firms in a variety of industries. We have described several ways in which the process was introduced—ways that reflect the culture of the firm. In chapter 10, we provide some guidelines for putting in place structures and practices to sustain a discovery-driven mindset.

ACTION STEPS

1. Think through the impetus factors that might cause your organization to be receptive to adopting DDP. Are there stalled growth projects that could be better handled? A history of failing to introduce innovations to the market in a timely way? New executives looking for fresh thinking? Summarize your conclusions in a short statement explaining "why we should adopt discovery-driven planning now."

2. Having clearly spelled out the answer to the question of why you should adopt this approach, next think about who the logical champions might be. Are there people who will gain disproportionately from adopting DDP as a consistent approach?

3. Think through your own list of potential benefits and beneficiaries for DDP. How will you get that first demonstration project or two?

4. Think through what kind of implementation approach makes the most sense, given your company and its culture. Support the champions trying to make it happen.

CHAPTER TEN

Sustaining
Discovery-Driven Growth

The challenge of introducing discovery-driven planning to an organization is by no means met just because a critical mass of people are using a few of the tools. We have found that certain structures and practices are necessary (if not entirely sufficient) to support the process and to sustain a discovery-driven mindset.

Structures and Practices

As Ron Pierantozzi of Air Products and Chemicals says, companies often don't realize that the ability to continuously drive innovation for the long term requires not just one competency but three: competencies

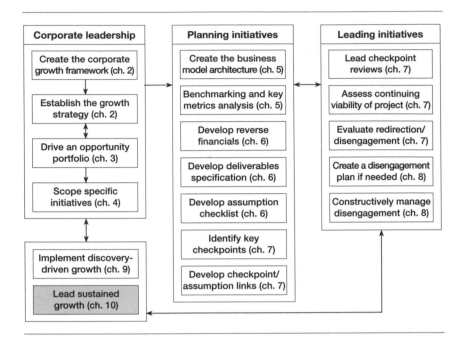

of discovery, which allow a firm to generate new ideas; competencies of incubation, which take an idea from an opportunity to a business proposition; and competencies of acceleration, which ramp up the business to stand on its own. We would add to these three one more, namely, competencies of disengagement and recycling, in which scarce and valuable innovative resources are pulled out of ventures or businesses that are stumbling and redirected toward more promising places.[1] These processes of sustaining discovery-driven growth have powerful implications for corporate leadership, as the shaded area on our road map suggests.

The Role of the CEO and Senior Team

In chapters 1 and 2, we began discussing the role of the CEO and senior team in terms of establishing the overall frame for the growth program and allocating responsibilities for executing it. Essentially, the senior team needs to create the right context, manage the portfolio of growth opportunities, reinforce (if not mandate) the company's fundamental approach to innovation, and commit to overseeing ventures with a discovery-driven mindset.

Setting Context

Setting the context within which everyone in the firm will pursue discovery-driven behavior calls for six sets of actions on the part of CEO and senior team.

1. *Agree on the most appropriate fundamental approach to innovation.*
   Given your company's culture and previous experience, the
   CEO and senior team need to decide which fundamental
   approach to innovation will make sense for the firm, because
   this fundamental approach will deeply affect the structure and
   processes of the overall growth program. Innosight and IBM's
   business strategy practice have developed an interesting tax-
   onomy of different approaches to innovation. As Wunker and
   Pohle report, each approach does best with a different
   management style:[2]

   - The "marketplace of ideas" approach allows staffers at all levels
     a great deal of leeway to experiment within the context of
     well-stated goals and boundaries and clear metrics for success.
     Wunker and Pohle cite Best Buy, 3M, Google, and media
     companies as examples. We might add Nokia to that list.
     Leaders play a support role here, but do not drive the inno-
     vation process top-down.

   - The "visionary leader" approach relies, as the name suggests,
     on a superbly talented and distinctive individual who drives
     innovation. Steve Jobs at Apple, Akio Morita at Sony, and

Anna Wintour at Vogue come to mind. Everybody in such a system plays a support role to the visionary.

- The "systematic innovation" approach encourages a few employees to undertake discrete venturing tasks within the context of the overall strategy and, with encouragement, to use cross-functional approaches. Examples include Procter & Gamble, Samsung, and Goldman Sachs. The senior team here plays a more hands-on role, shaping where resources are allocated and what the expectations are. In addition, corporate-wide resources such as brand are widely leveraged in this mold.

- The "collaborative innovation" approach leverages connections with external players, partners, and ecosystem members to drive innovation. Wunker and Pohle cite Vodafone and Facebook as examples. We'd be inclined to add to the list Sun Microsystems in its heyday.

While your company will have pockets of each type of innovation, the CEO needs to decide where the center of gravity for your approach is going to lie. For instance, a company that seeks to employ the marketplace-of-ideas approach will have to allocate relatively more resources to unproven or unknown concepts than would a more down-to-earth, systematic innovation type of firm.

2. *Decide on corporate growth objectives.* To establish a solid context, the senior team members first need to make sure that they themselves are clear about overall corporate objectives. Then they need to effectively communicate these objectives in actionable ways, as ESCO did in chapter 3. The key question is how much growth will come from the four growth categories: from core enhancements, from platform launches, from the three types of growth options, and also from acquisitions, including target margin and ROA growth in each category.

3. *Specify the growth framework—where to pursue growth and where not to do so.* It's also important to specify which *growth arenas* are acceptable and which are not in the quest for growth. The clearer you can be on the product market arenas in which you intend to grow, how you intend to grow, and how you hope to win, the more effectively people can execute against your growth objectives. Make sure your strategic logic is clear—in other words, clarify why your firm has elected to pursue the pattern of growth categories and arenas you have specified.

4. *Make appropriate resource allocations.* Third, the senior team is also responsible for *allocating* what proportions of the firm's resources will be dedicated to pursuing each growth category— allocating appropriate funding and staffing for core enhancements, platform launches, positioning options, scouting options, or stepping-stones, as well as for any acquisitions.

5. *Appoint, authorize, and set expectations for those executing.* Further growth-related decisions that a CEO or senior team member may be required to make include how growth will be governed, who will be involved, and who is going to drive the program management of growth. The senior team needs to set the context and expectations for those who are involved in venturing—from the growth board to venture governance structures to those driving the venturing program.

6. *Navigate the program.* Finally, although the CEO does not have to be the main driver, this executive is ultimately the custodian of the firm's growth mindset. Supporting this involves making sure that growth is always high on the firm's agenda (in spot number one, two, or three); making sure that human and financial resources are allocated to projects across time dimensions (from short-term core enhancements to long-term growth options); and setting up the opportunity generation, review, and

commitment processes, as well as supporting constructive disengagement and not penalizing intelligent failures.

Managing the Growth Portfolio

Managing the whole portfolio of initiatives in a firm is what ties together the dimensions of idea generation, incubation, acceleration, and discontinuation. Managing the portfolio across dimensions of uncertainty is critical not only to growth, but to building alignment between strategy, budgets, projects, and reward-and-incentive systems for people.

Different companies use different structures to do this work. In some companies, portfolio management sits with the strategy group. In others, it is the responsibility of the technical group. In still others, it lies with product development or venturing (sometimes called the portfolio management group). There is no one best spot.

Portfolio management, however, needs to accomplish three results. It needs to capture up-to-date information about initiatives and their progress, with appropriate redirection. It needs to actively engage the senior team as the portfolio unfolds and strategy is redirected in the face of unfolding reality. And finally, it needs to foster momentum. Options should move to platforms or the core fairly quickly or be discontinued; platforms should be moving toward the core to rejuvenate it.

Fortis venturing actually tracked the process of idea generation, vetting, screening, shutting down, and moving ventures forward. Kris Vander Velpen, head of the venturing group at Fortis, shared the group's data on this with us (figure 10-1). As the figure shows, although a company may screen multiple ideas, only a few make it through the "idea funnel" to become actual ventures.

Quite often, the process of managing a portfolio actively implies the need for organizational changes. At Swiss Re, for instance, the recognition that many new ideas cut across the traditional organizational structure prompted a major organizational change toward a matrix or-

FIGURE 10-1

The idea funnel at Fortis

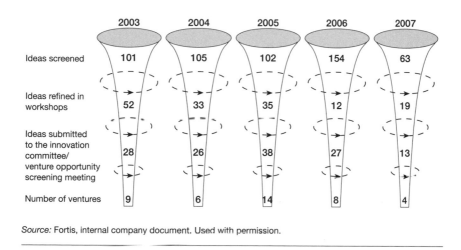

	2003	2004	2005	2006	2007
Ideas screened	101	105	102	154	63
Ideas refined in workshops	52	33	35	12	19
Ideas submitted to the innovation committee/ venture opportunity screening meeting	28	26	38	27	13
Number of ventures	9	6	14	8	4

Source: Fortis, internal company document. Used with permission.

ganization in 2006. At DuPont, the Knowledge-Intensive University (KIU) program ultimately resulted in the creation of entirely new growth platforms, which were reflected in a new organization. As Bob Cooper observed:

> One of our key initial learnings in running KIU was that very few market opportunities aligned with DuPont's internal, product/ technology-driven organization. We brought people from across the company with the needed skills to create growth concepts focusing on market opportunities in what we called the business builder session. Equally troublesome, however, was that the organization structure often stumbled in the execution phase. Accordingly, while DuPont senior leaders maintained the SBU structure, which focused on driving efficiencies in traditional products and technologies, they grouped the eighteen SBUs into five growth platforms that were market facing and led by very senior leaders. The platform goal was to grow the top line.

An example is the safety and protection platform that combined many of the safety-type product SBUs such as Kevlar and Tyvek. A specific success example from KIU and the new structure is the DuPont StormRoom introduced two years ago; the StormRoom is a room lined with Kevlar ballistic liner (behind the dry wall so the room is fully functional) designed to protect people from windblown debris during hurricanes and tornadoes. The Kevlar group had the technology and was going to sell just the fiber. The Tyvek organization, from its extensive work in house-wrap, had a deep knowledge of the home market in the U.S., as well as extensive relationships with major high-end builders. The combined group introduced the DuPont StormRoom, not just the fiber! A critical balance was reached here in a positive tension between driving efficiencies and shorter-term results, with big growth plays.[3]

Venture Governance: Growth Boards and Venture Boards

The purpose of a dedicated venture governance process is to make sure that ventures get the attention that they need from sufficiently senior people, are treated as an important corporate priority, and are managed with appropriate discipline.

A structure that generally works well is a high-level *growth board* that would weigh in on major resource commitments (such as committing to a platform launch) as well as manage the evolution of the overall growth process and pipeline. The board should meet regularly—at least once per quarter. It might have key executive team members or even the CFO or CEO in attendance, so that the board could make critical decisions on growth projects without the need for further approvals.

Venture boards, in contrast, would manage one or more specific initiatives. These boards can consist of one group or can be set up with different members for each venture. A typical venture board would consist of the venture leader, one or two peer venture leaders, representatives from the legal department and HR, and perhaps one or two executives from the core businesses. Among the tasks of this board is to facilitate the recycling and recouping of capabilities should the venture not work out. The venture board is also one mechanism through which resources elsewhere in the corporation can be mobilized to support the venture.

The venture boards meet at key checkpoints, as we described in chapter 7. These checkpoint reviews are intensely learning oriented. The venture team and board critically analyze what has been discovered, where the discoveries might apply, and how the venture should be redirected.

The venture board plays a major role in managing disengagement. As we articulated in chapter 8, ventures that are not working out need to be treated as valuable to the extent that something important has been learned—lessons that could be moved to a business, spun out, or added to another attempt on the market. It is this focus on learning at the *level below the level of the business* that differentiates firms that can fully exploit their venture program from those that do not. (As a side benefit, a well-run disengagement process helps deflect the performance pressures that often build up and precipitate expensive and destructive escalation of commitment to continuing a project in its original format, when in fact it should either be redirected or discontinued.)

As we mentioned in chapter 1, a practice that we have seen to be effective in resource allocation is to link projects' stage of development with the level of scrutiny they receive, the funding they are able to obtain, and the commitment from the organization. As we explained in chapter 7, Nokia has regularly done this, using what it called V milestones. A V0 stage venture could be just an idea that is allocated something on the order of 15,000 euros and some engineering time. The venture board would meet when the venture hit a critical checkpoint and determine whether it could go to the V1 stage. This would entitle the venture to more people and funding, perhaps as much as 150,000 euros. If the decision to move on to V1 was unfavorable, the venture would be stopped.

At the conclusion of the V1 stage, the venture board would next have to decide whether the project merited going to V2, at which point the concept would be launched and the risk and costs involved would increase exponentially, which meant a review by the growth board.

Notice how this technique accomplishes several goals. First, it sets a low bar to get a project going and therefore encourages experimentation. If failures occur, they occur early and cheaply, which accomplishes the second goal: conserving resources. Third, the technique ensures that ventures get thoroughly reviewed at two levels before they take on a life of their own.

The Product Development or Venturing Group

It's nearly impossible for breakthrough, white-space, or disruptive innovations to be run within an existing business unit.[4] As we've stressed throughout the book, highly uncertain endeavors need a different management approach than do established businesses, and it's therefore helpful if the uncertain projects are managed by a different group.

The group's mandate should, first of all, be clear. To avoid turf battles, you need to establish what kind of venturing should go on within the existing core business groups and what kind should take place in the venturing group. Typically, the types of investments we would call core enhancements get managed by the business groups, while ideas that cross business groups, call for radically different capabilities or technologies, or address different markets from the core business would be housed for a time in a new-venture division.

Venturing or growth-oriented groups with the following characteristics have tended to be more successful than others:

- First, they have a leader who is well networked horizontally across the firm as well as outside the firm. This person can not only identify where ideas and resources are, but also bring them together fruitfully.

- Second, the groups have a diverse membership: sales and operations experience is important. Some venture groups employ people who would not fit the mold of the established business, but who can provide great insight into new businesses.

- Third, membership in these groups is temporary, but it is not a revolving door. Ideally, a venturing group becomes a great spot for high-potential future leaders to spend some time, perhaps three years. The reason for this is that you don't want the venturing group to become a career destination—rather, you want the lessons learned about growth and change to grow the innovative capacity of the rest of the organization as well.

- Fourth, venture groups should be kept relatively lean in terms of resources. This will force them to be parsimonious and to avoid the temptation to let projects get too big too fast.

- Finally, venture groups should be connected to other parts of the company—to HR, to the legal and finance departments, and, of course, to the existing business groups—in order to facilitate the flow of ideas, people, capabilities, and technologies. In many cases we have observed, the real benefit of something discovered in a venturing group was that it improved the core business. It was critical that the venture did not become a standalone business.

From Venture to Launch

For ventures that have survived the incubation process and demonstrated that they are ready for prime time, the major turning point is the decision to launch. This usually involves substantive changes in how the venture is run. In our experience, it seldom works for the new venture division to try to accelerate growth platforms on its own.

Rather, in successful innovators such as IBM and Nokia, platform ventures are transferred to business groups to develop, or a new business group is formed from a combination of the venture and other units pulled out of business groups (a common practice with the EBOs at IBM). The reason for this is that you need to align the goals of the venture group with those of the core businesses, not lay the ground for bitter struggles over domain and resources.

At Air Products and Chemicals, for instance, Pierantozzi's new-business development team is kept small, its staff is diverse, and the people tend to rotate into and out of the group every few years. The group is explicitly set up in such a way that it could not take a business concept through to commercialization, because this ensures maximum flexibility up to the point at which a major venture is warranted. The firm maintains what it calls late-stage incubation accelerators within each growth platform or division. As a venture is ready to launch, the accelerators take over its active management. They are responsible for ramping up the business to growth and the final integration into a strategic business unit (or into a joint venture if a partnership is involved).

In contrast, another firm (unnamed to protect the guilty!) that struggles with its venturing program has no such concept of a temporary structure. Its teams set a business challenge and go after it with a ship-it-or-else mentality. Even though many of the ideas the people are working on are highly uncertain (and in reality, it would be almost impossible for even half of the ideas to succeed), when an innovation doesn't go as planned, the people involved feel like failures. Worse, the firm loses the ability to capitalize on the learning gained within the team, as the good people decamp to other organizations, their reputation permanently damaged by the "failure" they have worked on.

One last important aspect of preparing for launch is the concept of *prototyping*: practicing and testing before the launch is carried out. At Steelcase, for instance, the company is reported to actively practice all the necessary skills—from installation to technical support and sales—before even touching a single customer. That idea is entirely consistent with the whole notion of discovery first, action later.[5]

Discovery-Driven Growth: Your Opportunity?

A paradox that has long fascinated us is that established organizations seem so often to overlook incredible opportunities that in retrospect would seem to be a natural, easy extension of their existing businesses. Yet, often those vast, new growth opportunities are captured by firms from outside the industry or by entirely new companies. We've nevertheless also seen shining examples of companies that successfully got into new spaces—many of them described in this book. What makes the difference? Throughout the book, we've argued that it is using the right disciplines for different contexts. In their familiar, core businesses, companies have an arsenal of tools for driving efficiency, planning effectively, and coordinating their activities; everything from enterprise resource planning systems to Six Sigma supports these activities. But the effective companies have a different toolkit for approaching growth situations. In those situations, as we've shown throughout the book, you have to be just as disciplined, but the logic of success, failure, and progress is entirely different. The good news is that we have learned a lot about how to do this.

Where is your opportunity? Since most companies don't do a very effective job of growing over the long term, we think you can create an edge by getting just a bit better at avoiding things that will kill growth while you do a few more things that will support it.[6] Although a growth initiative sometimes requires a pretty substantial corporate overhaul (as we saw in the case of DuPont), it's often more a matter of shifting resources and attention in a more subtle way (as we saw with Air Products and Chemicals, Inc.). So there is no reason not to do some experimenting with some of the ideas we've presented here. For the most part, they are low-risk—after all, throughout the book we've emphasized keeping cost and risk contained until you know what you are doing.

We read about the Kodaks of the world every day, it seems: some company formerly at the top of its game stumbles, struggles, and is often eventually beaten in competition by an upstart, a more nimble competitor, or an entirely new solution to the problems it made its money solving. Throughout this book, we hope that we've convinced you that this does not have to be a foregone conclusion. Whereas the whole notion of sustainable competitive advantage is in fact a rare bird today, established organizations can survive in a world in which advantages are temporary.

But like any new skill, learning to thrive in high-uncertainty contexts requires a different approach from those you may be comfortable with. In particular, we hope that we have persuaded you to think differently about failure. Failure is a bad thing when it costs a lot, when it isn't intelligent, when you're repeating the same mistakes, or when it is covered up. Handled properly, intelligent failures may be among the most valuable experiences your organization can have. We also hope we've persuaded you to think differently about that other great goal of modern management: being right. In a new business, you can't and won't be right. So being right should never be a goal in and of itself. When things are supposed to be uncertain, the ability to predict accurately probably means that they weren't uncertain. And hitting your predictions every time probably means you are only doing the incremental things, not pursuing true breakthroughs.

For you, our readers, we'd like to close with some hopes for how what we (and many others) have learned about discovery-driven processes might be helpful.

If you happen to be a senior executive or CEO, the processes can give you a way to free up the creativity in your organization without going down the black hole of undisciplined innovation. You can empower, encourage, and help people to both think deeply and execute well without micromanaging them.

If you're a division head or someone running a business, give some thought to that stealth strategy of bringing discovery-driven principles to bear. You might soon find that growth becomes more conceivable and attainable once you do.

If you're a younger manager or an employee, perhaps just starting out, you can use these techniques to help yourself think more sharply and with more discipline about the things that your bosses are worried about.

If you're a person with a staff position or in an organization with a not-for-profit orientation, you can use the technique to build better business cases for the initiatives you believe to be important.

And for the potential entrepreneur in many of us, discovery-driven growth can provide a road map to a successful future business. Best of luck.

Notes

Chapter 1

1. J. B. Harreld, keynote speech, Strategic Management Society Annual Meeting, November 1–4, 2005, Orlando.

2. For background on these and other biases, see D. Kahneman, P. Slovic, and A. Tversky, *Judgment Under Uncertainty: Heuristics and Biases* (Cambridge and New York: Cambridge University Press, 1982); G. A. Miller, "The Magical Number Seven, Plus or Minus Two: Some Limits on Our Capacity for Processing Information," *Psychological Review* 63 (1956): 81–97; and R. Thaler, *The Winner's Curse: Paradoxes and Anomalies of Economic Life* (Princeton, NJ: Princeton University Press, 1982).

3. B. M. Staw and J. Ross, "Behavior in Escalation Situations: Antecedents, Prototypes and Solutions," *Research in Organizational Behavior* 9 (1987): 39–78; and B. M. Staw and J. Ross, "Knowing When to Pull the Plug," *Harvard Business Review* 65, no. 2 (1987): 68–74.

4. R. G. McGrath and I. C. MacMillan, "Discovery-Driven Planning," *Harvard Business Review* 73, no. 4 (1995): 44–54.

5. For examples of these prematurely championed practices, see P. Rosenzweig, *The Halo Effect . . . and the Eight Other Business Delusions That Deceive Managers* (New York: Free Press, 2007).

6. See, for example, J. B. Ayers, *Handbook of Supply Chain Management* (Boca Raton, FL: CRC Press, 2006); R. Burgelman and L. Valikangas, "Managing Internal Corporate Venturing Cycles," *Sloan Management Review* 46, no. 4 (2005): 26–34; J. C. Camillus, "Strategy As a Wicked Problem," *Harvard Business Review* 86, no. 5 (2008): 98–106; C. Christensen, S. Kaufman, and W. Shih, "Innovation Killers: How Financial Tools Destroy Your Capacity to Do New Things," *Harvard Business Review* 86, no. 1 (2008): 98–105, 137; C. M. Christensen, *The*

Innovator's Dilemma: When New Technologies Cause Great Firms to Fail (Boston: Harvard Business School Press, 1997); J. A. Dewar, *Assumption-Based Planning: A Tool for Reducing Avoidable Surprises* (Cambridge: Cambridge University Press, 2002); V. Govindarajan and C. Trimble, *Ten Rules for Strategic Innovators: From Idea to Execution* (Boston: Harvard Business School Press, 2005); and M. Rice, G. O'Connor, and R. Pierantozzi, "Implementing a Learning Plan to Counter Project Uncertainty," *MIT Sloan Management Review* 49, no. 2 (2008): 54–64; and D. Sull, "Disciplined Entrepreneurship," *MIT Sloan Management Review* 46, no. 1 (2004): 71–81.

7. R. D'Aveni, *Hypercompetition: Managing the Dynamics of Strategic Maneuvering* (New York: Free Press, 1994); I. C. MacMillan, "Controlling Competitive Dynamics by Taking Strategic Initiative," *Academy Management Executive* 2, no. 2 (1987): 111–118.

8. Christensen, Kaufman, and Shih, "Innovation Killers."

9. M. Baghai, S. Coley, and D. White, *The Alchemy of Growth: Practical Insights for Building the Enduring Enterprise* (New York: Perseus, 1999).

10. Govindarajan and Trimble, *Ten Rules for Strategic Innovators.*

11. Business Wire, "The NPD Group Reports on 2005 U.S. Toy Industry Sales," February 13, 2006, http://findarticles.com/p/articles/mi_m0EIN/is_/ai_n16061488.

12. To read the article that provoked this analysis, see Jon Ortiz, "Switching Tracks: Toy Store's Retro Concept Is Major Gamble," *Sacramento Bee*, May 28, 2006.

13. See "Sacramento City, California Statistics and Demographics (U.S. Census 2000)," AreaConnect Web page, http://sacramento.areaconnect.com/statistics.htm.

14. "Vanessa C.," review comment on Yelp, a user-review online network, December 12, 2007, www.yelp.com/biz/g-willikers-toy-emporium-sacramento. For the G. Willikers Toy Emporium, see www.gwillitoys.com.

15. S. Hamm and W. C. Symonds, "Kodak: Mistakes Made on the Road to Innovation," *BusinessWeek,* September 14, 2007.

Chapter 2

1. P. Burrows, "HP Says Goodbye to Drama," *BusinessWeek*, September 1, 2005, 83–86.

2. Data from "Financial Statements for Hewlett-Packard Co.," *BusinessWeek*, http://investing.businessweek.com/research/stocks/financials/financials.asp?bridgesymbol=US;HPQ.

3. J. Kirby and T. A. Stewart, "The Institutional Yes: Interview with Jeff Bezos of Amazon.com," *Harvard Business Review* 85, no. 10 (2007): 75–82.

4. Microsoft and Windows are either registered trademarks or trademarks of Microsoft Corporation in the United States and/or other countries.

5. D. J. Collis and M. G. Rukstad, "Can You Say What Your Strategy Is?" *Harvard Business Review* 86, no. 4 (2008): 82–90.

6. B. Lovas and S. Ghoshal, "Strategy As Guided Evolution," *Strategic Management Journal* 21, no. 9 (2000): 875–896.

7. A. Goldstein, "TI's Rock Amid Rubble," *Chief Executive*, November 1, 2001.

8. R. Cooper, "Leadership Development Program: Knowledge-Intensive Growth at DuPont," *Wharton Leadership Digest* 4, no. 10 (2000).

9. I. C. MacMillan, and R. G. McGrath, "Managing Growth Through Corporate Venturing," in *Entrepreneurship: The Engine of Growth*, vol. 3, *Place*, ed. M. P. Rice and T. G. Habbershon (Westport, CT: Greenwood Publishing, 2007), 21–48.

10. Cooper, "Leadership Development Program."

11. R. Cooper, "Conquering a Culture of Stagnation" (presentation at Crouching Tiger, Hidden Opportunity, the IMI Annual Conference; Irish Management Institute, Druid's Glenn, Ireland, April 2005).

12. R. Burgelman and L. Valikangas, "Managing Internal Corporate Venturing Cycles," *Sloan Management Review* 46, no. 4 (2005): 26–34; C. M. Christensen and M. E. Raynor, *"The Innovator's Solution: Creating and Sustaining Successful Growth* (Boston: Harvard Business School, 2003); V. Govindarajan and C. Trimble, *Ten Rules for Strategic Innovators: From Idea to Execution* (Boston: Harvard Business School Press, 2005); and J. B. Harreld, C. O'Reilly, and M. L. Tushman, "Dynamic Capabilities at IBM: Driving Strategy into Action," *California Management Review* 49, no. 4 (2007): 21–43.

13. For more on the KIU process, see Corporate Strategy Board, *Aligning Goals and Resources: Translating Strategy into Action* (Washington, DC: Corporate Executive Board, 2005), 97–125.

14. R. Cooper, "Supercharging Growth by Leveraging Your Firm's Capabilities," working paper, Snider Entrepreneurial Center, The Wharton School, Philadelphia, 2004.

15. Ibid.

16. C. Andriadis, "DuPont Group Vice President Briefs Investors on Business Growth in Safety and Protection . . ." Reuters, May 21, 2008, available at www.reuters.com/article/pressRelease/idUS169777+21-May-2008+PRN20080521.

17. R. G. McGrath and I. C. MacMillan, *MarketBusters: 40 Strategic Moves That Drive Exceptional Business Growth* (Boston: Harvard Business School Press, 2005), chapter 7.

18. C. Gutierrez, "DuPont's Emerging Market Solution," Forbes.com, January 9, 2008, available at www.forbes.com/2008/01/09/dupont-emerging-closer-equity-cx_cg_0109markets37.html.

19. Among the tools the team used were ideas from our previous book, Mc-Grath and MacMillan, *MarketBusters*, which focuses extensively on the challenges of generating new ideas. We would refer this book to readers who'd like tools for idea generation.

Chapter 3

1. R. G. McGrath and I. C. MacMillan, *The Entrepreneurial Mindset: Strategies for Continuously Creating Opportunity in an Age of Uncertainty* (Boston: Harvard Business School Press, 2000).

2. P. Burrows and J. Greene, "Yes, Steve, You Fixed It. Congrats! Now What's Act Two?" *BusinessWeek*, July 31, 2000, cover story.

3. G. Colvin, "Selling P&G," *Fortune*, September 18, 2007.

4. E. H. Bowman and D. Hurry, "Strategy Through the Option Lens: An Integrated View of Resource Investments and the Incremental-Choice Process," *Academy of Management Review*, 18, no. 4 (1993): 760–783; A. K. Dixit and R. S. Pindyck, *Investment Under Uncertainty* (Princeton, NJ: Princeton University Press, 1994); R. G. McGrath, "Falling Forward: Real Options Reasoning and Entrepreneurial Failure," *Academy of Management Review* 24 (1999): 13–30; A. B. v. Putten and I. C. MacMillan, "Making Real Options Really Work," *Harvard Business Review* 82, no. 12 (2004): 134.

5. T. Keil, R. G. McGrath, and T. Tukiainen, "Gems from the Ashes: Capability Creation and Transformation in Internal Corporate Venturing," *Organization Science* (in press).

6. R. G. McGrath and T. Keil, "The Value Captor's Process: Getting the Most Out of Your New Business Ventures," *Harvard Business Review* 85, no. 5 (2007).

7. M. Sawhney and R. Wolcott, "The Seven Myths of Innovation," *Financial Times* (London), September 24, 2004.

8. "Boeing Teams with Canadian Firm to Build Heavy-Lift Rotorcraft," press release, Boeing, St. Louis, July 8, 2008, available at www.boeing.com/news/releases/2008/q3/080708c_nr.html.

9. E. M. Gillespie, "Amazon Tops Forecasts, Projects Continued Growth," *USA Today*, July 27, 2005.

10. See, for example, C. Holahan, "Auctions on eBay: A Dying Breed," *BusinessWeek*, June 3, 2008

11. "Putting Theory to Work at DuPont," *Wharton Alumni Magazine*, winter volume, 2007.

Chapter 4

1. See M. Treacy and J. Sims, "Take Command of Your Growth," *Harvard Business Review* 82, no. 4 (2004): 127–133, on this point.

2. R. G. McGrath and T. Keil, "The Value Captor's Process: Getting the Most Out of Your New Business Ventures," *Harvard Business Review* 85, no. 5 (2007): 128–136.

3. Z. Block and I. C. MacMillan, *Corporate Venturing: Creating New Businesses Within the Firm* (Boston: Harvard Business School Press, 1993); C. M. Christensen and M. E. Raynor, *The Innovator's Solution: Creating And Sustaining Successful Growth* (Boston: Harvard Business School, 2003); V. Govindarajan and C. Trimble, *Ten Rules for Strategic Innovators: From Idea to Execution* (Boston: Harvard Business School Press, 2005); J. B. Harreld, C. O'Reilly, and M. L. Tushman, "Dynamic Capabilities at IBM: Driving Strategy into Action," *California Management Review* 49, no. 4 (2007): 21–43; C. O'Reilly and M. L. Tushman, "The Ambidextrous Organization," *Harvard Business Review* 82, no. 4 (2004): 74.

4. M. L. Tushman and C. O'Reilly, "Ambidextrous Organizations: Managing Evolutionary and Revolutionary Change," *California Management Review* 38, no. 4 (1996): 8.

5. Harreld, O'Reilly, and Tushman, "Dynamic Capabilities at IBM."

6. Uwe E. Reinhardt, "Perspectives on the Pharmaceutical Industry," *Health Affairs* 20, no. 5 (2001): 136–149, available at www.npcnow.org/resources/PDFs/reinhardt.pdf.

Chapter 5

1. G. Friedman, "The History of Prepaid Phone Cards," Long Distance Post, LLC, Web page, www.ldpost.com/telecom-articles/The-History-of-Prepaid-Phone-Cards.html.

2. D. Desjardins, "Observers Raise Eyebrows over Blockbuster's Bold Moves," *DSN Retailing Today*, 44 (2005): 6.

3. M. Honan, "Photo Essay: Unlikely Places Where *Wired* Pioneers Had Their *Eureka!* Moments," *Wired Magazine*, March 24, 2008.

4. M. Lindow, "Fee Changes Helped Propel DVD Rental Company to Fast Growth," *Silicon Valley/San Jose Business Journal*, November 23, 2001.

5. Netflix, Annual Report, 2003.

6. Data from Netflix corporate page, www.ir.netflix.com, and annual reports.

7. Thomas F. Schuler, telephone interview with author (R. G. McGrath), July 16, 2007.

8. D. Edgar, "From Data, to Insight, to Execution: A DuPont Knowledge Intensity University Case Study," case study (University Park, PA: Institute for the Study of Business Markets, Pennsylvania State University, 2004).

9. Schuler, interview.

10. Ibid.

11. H. Rubin, "The Nursing Home Industry and Health Care Spending," July 8, 2007, www.therubins.com/homes/hospitiind.htm.

12. For more on these ideas and questions, we strongly recommend that readers see C. Christensen, S. D. Anthony, and E. A. Roth, *Seeing What's Next: Using the Theories of Innovation to Predict Industry Change* (Boston: Harvard Business School Press, 2004).

13. M. L. Katz and C. Shapiro, "Network Externalities, Competition, and Compatibility," *American Economic Review* 75, no. 3 (1985): 424–440; M. Schilling, "Technology Success and Failure in Winner-Take-All Markets: The Impact of Learning Orientation, Timing, and Network Externalities," *Academy of Management Journal* 45, no. 2 (2002): 387–398.

14. R. G. McGrath and I. C. MacMillan, *MarketBusters: 40 Strategic Moves That Drive Exceptional Business Growth* (Boston: Harvard Business School Press, 2005).

15. J. Alexander, *Performance Dashboards and Analysis for Value Creation* (Hoboken, NJ: Wiley, 2006).

16. For the use of key metrics by executives, see R. S. Kaplan and D. P. Norton, "Mastering the Management System," *Harvard Business Review* 86, no. 1 (2008): 62–73.

17. G. B. Stewart, *The Quest for Value* (New York: Collins Business, 1991).

18. McGrath and MacMillan, *MarketBusters*.

Chapter 7

1. Z. Block and I. C. MacMillan, "Milestones for Successful Venture Planning," *Harvard Business Review* 63, no. 5 (1985): 84–90; Z. Block and I. C. MacMillan, *Corporate Venturing: Creating New Businesses Within the Firm* (Boston: Harvard Business School Press, 1993).

2. T. Tukiainen, *The Unexpected Benefits of Internal Corporate Ventures: An Empirical Examination of the Consequences of Investment in Corporate Ventures* (Espoo, Finland: Helsinki University of Technology, 2004).

3. R. G. McGrath and T. Keil, "The Value Captor's Process: Getting the Most Out of Your New Business Ventures," *Harvard Business Review* 85, no. 5 (2007): 128–136; R. Sethi and Z. Iqbal, "Stage-Gate Controls, Learning Failure, and Adverse Effect on Novel New Products," *Journal of Marketing* 72, no. 1 (2008): 118–134.

4. S. Thomke, "R&D Comes to Service: Bank of America's Pathbreaking Experiments," *Harvard Business Review* 81, no. 4 (2003): 70.

5. Thomas F. Schuler, telephone interview with author (R. G. McGrath), July 17, 2007.

6. For inspiration, see our previous book on finding opportunities: R. G. McGrath and I. C. MacMillan, *MarketBusters: 40 Strategic Moves That Drive Exceptional Business Growth* (Boston: Harvard Business School Press, 2005).

Chapter 8

1. N. F. Matta and R. N. Ashkenas, "Why Good Projects Fail Anyway," *Harvard Business Review* 81, no. 9 (2003): 109–114.

2. G. A. Stevens and J. Burley, "3000 Raw Ideas: 1 Commercial Success!" *Research Technology Management* 40, no. 3 (1997): 16–27.

3. S. B. Sitkin, "Learning Through Failure: The Strategy of Small Losses," in *Research in Organizational Behavior*, ed. B. M. Staw and L. L. Cummings (Greenwich, CT: JAI Press, 1992), 14: 231–266.

4. R. G. McGrath and T. Keil, "The Value Captor's Process: Getting the Most out of Your New Business Ventures," *Harvard Business Review* 85, no. 5 (2007): 128–136.

5. J. Ross and B. M. Staw, "Expo 86: An Escalation Prototype," *Administrative Science Quarterly* 31 (1986): 274–297; B. M. Staw, "Knee-Deep in the Big Muddy: A Study of Escalating Commitment to a Chosen Course of Action," *Organizational Behavior and Human Performance* 16, no. 1 (1976): 27–44; B. M. Staw and J. Ross, "Knowing When to Pull the Plug," *Harvard Business Review* 65, no. 2 (1987): 68–74.

6. Ross and Staw, "Expo 86"; J. Ross and B. M. Staw, "Organizational Escalation and Exit: Lessons from the Shoreham Nuclear Power Plant," *Academy of Management Journal* 36, no. 4 (1993): 701–732; Staw, "Knee-Deep in the Big Muddy"; B. M. Staw and J. Ross, "Behavior in Escalation Situations: Antecedents, Prototypes and Solutions," *Research in Organizational Behavior* 9 (1987): 39–78.

7. McGrath and Keil, "The Value Captor's Process."

8. G. R. Sullivan and M. V. Harper, *Hope Is Not a Method: What Business Leaders Can Learn from America's Army* (New York: Broadway Books, 1997).

9. McGrath and Keil, "The Value Captor's Process."

10. M. A. Maidique and B. Zirger, "The New Product Learning Cycle," *Research Policy* 14, no. 6 (1985): 299–313.

Chapter 9

1. Former head of Nokia's New Ventures Organization, telephone interview with authors, November 9, 2005 (name withheld to protect privacy), referring

to R. G. McGrath and I. C. MacMillan, *The Entrepreneurial Mindset: Strategies for Continuously Creating Opportunity in an Age of Uncertainty* (Boston: Harvard Business School Press, 2000).

2. G. Hamel, "Bringing Silicon Valley Inside," *Harvard Business Review* (September–October 1999): 70–84.

3. B. Leleu, "Fortis Venturing (A): Building the Fighting Spirit," case IMD-3-1276 (Lausanne, Switzerland: International Institute for Management Development, 2003), 7.

4. B. Hindo, "At 3M, a Struggle Between Efficiency and Creativity," *BusinessWeek*, June 11, 2007.

5. M. Baghai, S. Coley, and D. White, *The Alchemy of Growth: Practical Insights for Building the Enduring Enterprise* (New York: Perseus, 1999).

6. For more on EBO, we recommend A. Deutschman, "Building a Better Skunk Works," *Fast Company* 92 (2005): 68–69.

7. Anonymous, telephone interview with authors, December 2004. All subsequent quotations not ascribed to specific people are from our personal interviews of business leaders who wished to remain anonymous. These interviews were conducted between 2001 and 2007.

8. To learn more about strategic learning forums, see M. L. Tushman et al., "Relevance and Rigor: Executive Education as a Lever in Shaping Practice and Research," *Academy of Management Learning and Education* 6, no. 3 (2007): 345–332.

9. For more on venturing practices at Nokia, see R. G. McGrath, T. Keil, and T. Tukiainen, "Extracting Value from Corporate Venturing," *Sloan Management Review* 48, no. 1 (2006): 50–56.

10. Ron Pierantozzi, telephone interview with author (R. G. McGrath), June 6, 2006. Subsequent quotations are also from this interview.

11. For a discussion on attacking these negative forces through DRAT (delay and resistance analysis table), see R. G. McGrath and I. C. MacMillan, *MarketBusters: 40 Strategic Moves That Drive Exceptional Business Growth* (Boston: Harvard Business School Press, 2005).

Chapter 10

1. For additional insight on the competencies required to manage an entire pipeline of innovative ideas, see R. G. McGrath and T. Keil, "The Value Captor's Process: Getting the Most out of Your New Business Ventures," *Harvard Business Review* 85, no. 5 (2007); Z. Block and I. C. MacMillan, *Corporate Venturing: Creating New Businesses Within the Firm* (Boston: Harvard Business School Press, 1993); V. Govindarajan and C. Trimble, *Ten Rules for Strategic Innovators:*

From Idea to Execution (Boston: Harvard Business School Press, 2005); M. T. Hansen and J. Birkinshaw, "The Innovation Value Chain," *Harvard Business Review* 85, no. 6 (2007): 121–130.

2. S. Wunker and G. Pohle, "Built for Innovation," *Forbes*, November 12, 2007, 137–143.

3. Robert Cooper, "Conquering a Culture of Stagnation" (presentation at the Irish Management Institute Annual Conference, "Crouching Tiger, Hidden Opportunity," Druid's Glenn, Ireland, 2005).

4. C. M. Christensen and M. E. Raynor, *The Innovator's Solution: Creating and Sustaining Successful Growth* (Boston: Harvard Business School, 2003).

5. J. P. Hackett, "Preparing for the Perfect Product Launch," *Harvard Business Review* 85, no. 4 (2007): 45–50.

6. R. Foster and S. Kaplan, *Creative Destruction: Why Companies That Are Built to Last Underperform the Market—And How to Successfully Transform Them* (New York: Doubleday, 2001); C. Markides, *All the Right Moves* (Boston: Harvard Business School Press, 2001).

Index

About the Authors

Rita Gunther McGrath, an associate professor at Columbia Business School in New York, is one of the world's leading experts on strategic business growth in highly uncertain environments. She works with both Global 1,000 icons and smaller but fast-growing organizations. Her current clients include Air Products and Chemicals, Inc., Nokia, Microsoft, AXA Equitable, Novartis, Swiss Re, Glanbia, ON2 Technologies, and the World Economic Forum. She is a popular speaker and works extensively with senior leadership teams.

She has coauthored two previous books: *The Entrepreneurial Mindset* (2000) and *MarketBusters: 40 Strategic Moves That Drive Exceptional Business Growth* (2005), published by Harvard Business Press. *Market-Busters* has been translated into ten languages and was named one of the best business books of 2005 by *strategy+business*. It was featured by Bill Gates at the 2005 Microsoft CEO Summit, whose theme "New Pathways to Growth" was derived from the book's main topic.

Rita has appeared on television and radio and has been interviewed by numerous publications, including the *Wall Street Journal*, *New York Times*, *Financial Times*, *BusinessWeek*, *Inc.*, and *Entrepreneur*. She blogs actively on strategic growth (see www.ritamcgrath.com) and is featured as a discussion leader at Harvard Business Online (see http://discussionleader .hbsp.com/mcgrath/). She has coauthored six articles in the *Harvard*

Business Review, including the best-selling "Discovery-Driven Planning," which has been highly recommended by Clayton Christensen.

Rita joined the faculty of Columbia Business School in 1993. Prior to life in academia, she was an IT director, worked in the political arena, and founded two start-ups. Her PhD is from the Wharton School, University of Pennsylvania. At Columbia, she teaches MBA and Executive MBA courses in strategy and growth. She teaches regularly in Columbia's top-rated executive education programs and is the Faculty Director for *Leading Strategic Growth and Change* and *Creating Strategy, Tokyo.*

Rita's academic publications have appeared in leading journals such as the *Strategic Management Journal, Academy of Management Review, Academy of Management Journal,* and *Management Science.* She has won numerous awards for excellence in scholarship. Among these are the Strategic Management Society Best Paper and runner-up awards in 2001 and 2004, respectively; the Maurice Holland Award from the Industrial Research Institute; the *Academy of Management Review* Best Paper Award, and the Entrepreneurship Theory and Practice Award for the Best Conceptual Paper (both 1992 and 1996). She is on several editorial boards of prestigious journals.

Ian C. MacMillan is the Academic Director for the Sol C. Snider Entrepreneurial Research Center at the Wharton School, University of Pennsylvania. He is also the Dhirubhai Ambani Professor of Innovation and Entrepreneurship. Formerly he was Director of the Entrepreneurial Center at New York University and a professor at Columbia and Northwestern Universities and the University of South Africa. In 1999 he was awarded the Swedish Foundation for Small Business Research Prize for his contribution to research in entrepreneurship.

Prior to joining the academic world, MacMillan was a chemical engineer and gained experience in gold and uranium mining, chemical and explosives manufacturing, oil refining, and soap and food production; he was also a scientist at the South African Atomic Energy Board. He has been a director of several companies in the travel, import/export, and pharmaceutical industries. He also has extensive consulting experience, having worked with such companies as Air Products, DuPont, General Electric, Microsoft, IBM, Citibank, Chubb & Son, Texas Instruments, KPMG, Hewlett-Packard, Intel, Fluor Daniel, Matsushita (Japan), Olympus (Japan), and L. G. Group (South Korea), among others.

MacMillan's articles have appeared in the *Harvard Business Review*, *Sloan Management Review*, *Journal of Business Venturing*, *Administrative Science Quarterly*, *Academy of Management Journal*, *Academy of Management Review*, *Academy of Management Executive*, *Management Science*, *Strategic Management Journal*, *Research and Technology Management*, and other publications.

YOUR DISCOVERY-DRIVEN TOOLKIT—FREE ONLINE

To help you create your own discovery-driven organization, authors Rita McGrath and Ian MacMillan have developed a suite of online resources to better identify, manage, and leverage your company's opportunities. These four FREE multimedia tools will help put the ideas in this book to work for you.

AUDIO
Hear the Experts Speak

Growth can really be a predictable, manageable, and disciplined process in your organization. In this audio lesson the authors tell you how to start putting discovery-driven practices to work.

TOOL
The Discovery-Driven Model

Move from "conventional" to "breakthrough" thinking more easily—thanks to a practical reference that illustrates the differences in nine critical areas of management.

QUIZ
How Discovery-Driven Are You?

This brief survey will identify the particular mindset issues that are likely to get in your way—then redirect you toward greater success.

VIDEO
The First Step Is Planning

Author Rita McGrath shows how you can start pursuing dynamic growth with confidence: It begins with building discovery-driven planning into your strategy.

 DOWNLOAD THESE FREE TOOLS AT
www.DiscoveryDrivenGrowth.com/resources